'Debbie and Anna provide not only insp[...] also offer a step-by-step guide as to ho[...] careers. Central to the book is the most i[...] women we need to support and champi[...] top. A sisterhood is the key to success.'
Nicola Mendelsohn, VP of EMEA

'Women are incredible and can achieve anything if they put their minds to it, and women supporting other women is the key to our success. We need more women leading businesses, and this book will help to inspire women to reach the top.'
Kelly Hoppen, proprietor of Kelly Hoppen Interiors

'As a proud feminist I believe we must do all we can to remove any barriers to women's success and to unlock their full potential, and Debbie's passion to equip women with the confidence and skills to reach the top in their careers is truly inspiring.'
Sadiq Khan, Mayor of London

'I loved this book and the message behind it – I'm passionate about the women in my life, and really believe that the way to promote women in all kinds of business is the way to equality. This is a really hands-on guide to working out what you want and the practical steps to getting it.'
Melissa Hemsley, author of *The Art of Eating Well*, *Good + Simple* and *Eat Happy*

'I have always been lucky to have a strong base of female friends in my business and we give each other advice on everything from working motherhood to navigating office politics. *Believe, Build, Become* astutely identifies that this female solidarity is fundamental to success and equality. This is an important book with a crucial message.'
Nancy Josephson, Partner, WME

'It is so important to instil these values in women. This knowledge is great power and will gift its reader the autonomy they need and deserve.'
Jameela Jamil, actress, model, presenter and activist

'We all have those moments of doubt, and that's when we need our sisterhood to have our backs, not just as a support network, but as cheerleaders too. This is the central message behind *Believe, Build, Become*, and something I passionately believe in. If we want to see a world where women are in an equal number of top jobs as men, then it's essential that we propel each other forward and support each other. Men have been doing it for years; it's time for women to do the same. As Debbie and Anna say, the sisterhood works.'
Farrah Storr, editor-in-chief of *Cosmopolitan*

About the Authors

Debbie Wosskow OBE is recognised as one of the most prominent successful serial entrepreneurs in the UK. She is the current London *Evening Standard* 'Entrepreneur of the Year' – awarded to her for her work in scaling businesses. Debbie was the founder of Love Home Swap, sold to Wyndham Destination Network for $53 million in July 2017. Following this exit, she co-founded AllBright with Anna Jones.

Debbie authored the independent UK government review of the sharing economy and was the founding chair of Sharing Economy UK. She sits on the Mayor of London's Business Advisory Board and is a board member of the Women's Prize for Fiction.

Hailing from a family of female entrepreneurs, her entrepreneurial journey started at the age of 25 when Debbie launched her first company Mantra, a communications consultancy, later sold to Loewy Group in 2007.

Debbie was awarded an OBE for services to business in 2017. She graduated with an MA in Philosophy and Theology from New College, Oxford.

Anna Jones is an experienced CEO and board advisor, renowned as a prominent and progressive leader in the media and marketing sector. She has a particular interest in female empowerment.

Anna is the former CEO at Hearst UK, where she led a period of transformation in the business. She expanded the reach of the world-famous magazine group through strategic diversification, growing digital audiences, and developing events and licensing divisions.

Anna is on the board of the Creative Industries Federation and was a NED at Telecom Italia. She has been shortlisted for Media Pioneer of the Year at the British Media Awards.

Anna graduated with a BA in International Business Management from Newcastle University's Business School. She took the leap from the corner office to co-founder of AllBright in 2017 and is enjoying the entrepreneurial white-knuckle ride.

AllBright aims to help women build the network, skills and confidence that they need to thrive in their careers. It combines members clubs for women, opened in both the UK and the US, with a digital academy, supporting female founders, executives and consultants.

Debbie Wosskow and Anna Jones

BELIEVE
BUILD
BECOME

HOW TO **SUPERCHARGE** YOUR CAREER

1 3 5 7 9 10 8 6 4 2

Virgin Books, an imprint of Ebury Publishing,
20 Vauxhall Bridge Road,
London SW1V 2SA

Virgin Books is part of the Penguin Random House group of companies
whose addresses can be found at global.penguinrandomhouse.com

Penguin
Random House
UK

First published in the United Kingdom by Virgin Books in 2019

www.penguin.co.uk

A CIP catalogue record for this book is available from the British Library

ISBN 9780753554012

Typeset in 11/16pt Sabon LT Std
by Integra Software Services Pvt. Ltd, Pondicherry

Printed and bound in Great Britain by Clays Ltd, Elcograf S.p.A.

Penguin Random House is committed to a sustainable future for our
business, our readers and our planet. This book is made from Forest
Stewardship Council® certified paper.

Contents

Introduction

We first met each other at a party in 2015, introduced by someone who said, 'You two should be friends.' And over that initial gin and tonic – and the breakfasts and dinners that followed – we realised that we were two strangers thinking the same thing. In an age where feminism is plastered on T-shirts, pop stars routinely sing about female empowerment and women are more likely than men to go on to higher education, why were there still so few women leading in business?

We came together at a point where we'd both had 20 years in the world of work, and despite having taken very different paths – Debbie as an entrepreneur and Anna as an executive in corporations rising to the top job of CEO – we both still saw around the same number of women at the top as when we started in the late 1990s.

How had nothing changed?

As we discussed the topic more, we found out we had similar backgrounds: we were both raised by strong women with mothers and grandmothers who worked; we did well at school and university and then crashed with a shock into the world of work, expecting the equality we were brought up with but instead finding that the real world was very different. The world of business was – and still is – controlled by men for men. The statistics make for depressing reading. In the world of entrepreneurship, only one in five businesses in the UK have female founders and female-run businesses only attract around 2 per cent of venture capital funding in the UK and US. In the corporate world the glass ceiling is still very much intact: in the US, only 4.8 per cent of CEOs of Fortune 500 companies are women; in the UK there are now only six CEOs of FTSE 100 companies, and globally women account for less than a quarter (24 per cent) of senior roles, according to Catalyst data.

And yet, 'Data shows that women CEOs in the Fortune 1000 drove three times the returns compared to S&P 500 enterprises run predominantly by men,' says Craig Newmark, advisor to Women Who Tech, a Washington-based initiative. Meanwhile, a spokesman for the UK government suggested untapped female entrepreneurship 'may be the greatest economic opportunity of the twenty-first century'. It literally pays – for business and indeed for society – to have women at the top.

So why were there so few of us leading companies? We had both worked with extraordinary women who we'd seen held back by invisible forces. As we chatted, we realised that for us, enough was enough. Now we had reached positions where we could do something about it, we needed to help change the conversation. Because change needed to happen, and it needed to start now. Neither of us wanted to see our young daughters enter a workforce where these barriers still exist.

As we picked apart our very different routes to success – Debbie's as a multiple business founder, with her last business Love Home Swap selling for $53 million, and Anna's as the CEO of Hearst magazines, a company with a 100-year history of selling magazines to women, but never having a woman in the CEO's chair – we realised there was a common theme. It is within the power of other women to help empower, improve and give you a leg-up, just as old boys' networks have been doing for men for centuries.

We call it the 'sisterhood'. We are happy reclaiming that 1970s feminist and campaigning term. For us, it's about the gang of women who help build you up and believe in you so you become something even greater than you were at the beginning. It's not just a support network, although that's an important function, and we're sure you have your own group of women in your personal life who act in this way. Instead the work sisterhood is a group of women who can be your own personal board of advisors; women you can turn to when you've got tough business decisions to make, who can prompt you to take that risk or put yourself forward for promotion. It's people who share their own networks to help push you up the ladder – and you do the same for them in return.

We had both relied on our own sisterhoods to take us to the top of our respective fields, and we continued to empower and improve one another in all aspects of our lives as entrepreneurs. What we're really good at is making each other better every day. We constantly challenge each other, tweak each other's plans and ambitions and use the other as a sounding board.

Many of our most successful female friends and business contacts, who you will read about in this book, say the same thing. The sisterhood has been crucial to their success. When we conducted wider research into the topic, we found that it's really true: the higher up women are in an organisation, the more likely they are to have a broad sisterhood. You need the sisterhood in every step of your business journey, whether you are fresh from education or already making waves at the top – in fact, in our experience, it can be lonely as a woman at the top, so you need a sisterhood even more when you think you've made it.

While we call it the 'sisterhood', we very much include enlightened men in there, too. Some amazing men have played a huge part in helping us both get to where we are today, from promoting us to investing in our businesses and generally believing in us. Yes, the system is flawed, but the answer isn't *just* to get angry; we need men on the journey of change – and the most enlightened also want to see that change happen.

There are deep societal forces that are responsible for the dearth of women at the top, and there are initiatives, enterprises and legislation in place to help start to address some of this. That's brilliant, and it needs to keep happening. But when we sat and thought about all this, in the months after we met, we focused on how we could help women who want to succeed do it for themselves. There has to be both a push and a pull.

There is a quote by Madeleine Albright that was very much the inspiration behind what we do: 'There is a special place in hell for women who don't help other women'. We think everyone should try to earn a special place in heaven by helping another woman out. This is the reason we founded AllBright in 2017 – to create physical spaces alongside a digital network for women to help them gain the skills, confidence and connections needed to achieve their goals. The women who use our clubs in the UK and the US say that having a physical space to work and connect with like-minded women is important to them – while the thousands of women who have studied with us on our free, online 10-week AllBright Academy say that the skills we teach in the programme have given them the confidence to either launch a business or propel themselves higher up the corporate ladder. Watching what we've created help other women achieve their business and career dreams has been the most fulfilling journey of our careers.

This is why we wanted to spread the message further with this book. Our mantra at AllBright is 'sisterhood works' and we truly believe it. It might look effortless from the outside, but we meticulously game every meeting, we plan every pitch and then we practise, practise, practise with each other; all of our best 'off the cuff remarks' are rehearsed. It is a lot of work, but it *works*.

So we've enlisted the support of some of the amazing women in our sisterhood across many industries, from the actress Naomie Harris to businesswoman and tech founder Whitney Wolfe Herd to interior designer Kelly Hoppen to top civil servant Antonia Romeo, as well as businesswoman Anastasia Soare – the 'Eyebrow Queen' – who arrived in America as an immigrant and built a billion-dollar business from scratch. We've taken our experience in our two separate fields and asked others for theirs, to provide inspiration from many walks of life.

Alongside that, there are actual practical real-world tips about how to succeed in business whatever sector or stage you're at, from those starting out in their career like gal-dem founder Liv Little (who has already built a business out of hard graft and networking at the age of 24) to those with years of experience like Karen Blackett, one of the most powerful women in British advertising. The experience of our collective sisterhood is woven into the DNA of this book. We are both very much hands-on, practical people (we're northerners after all!) and believe in the power of doing, so we've included worksheets to help you practise with someone from your own work sisterhood to build up your skills. These exercises are a career-long process – something we've done our whole business lives, and continue to do. As you change and develop, so you will need to keep re-evaluating what's important to you and where you need to improve.

As you read on, you'll discover there are three parts to this book. The first section *Believe* is all about believing in yourself from the inside out. This starts by working out what the components are that make up 'Project You': your strengths, your weaknesses, your motivations and your goals. Naomie Harris is fascinating on how she's had to mine her strengths in her work as an actress, something we can all learn from, while Anastasia Soare talks about her dual motivations – to be something significant coupled with the very relatable drive to make money as a single mother.

A huge part of believing in yourself is working on that gnarly issue of confidence, something we see lets women down time and time again. We'll see that crises of confidence happen to everyone. The Paralympic-medal-winning athlete Baroness Tanni Grey-Thompson has said that, despite competing in front of a global audience, when she had to do her maiden speech in the House of Lords, she actually threw up from nerves. There are lots of ways to combat these feelings and we've got a 10-step confidence plan to help you prepare for those moments.

The final thing we think is important to believing in yourself and succeeding is tapping into that entrepreneurial mindset. If you feel scared and clueless, don't worry, Sahar Hashemi, co-founder of Coffee Republic says that's a huge advantage. Why? Well, you'll have to read on.

Once we've got you believing in yourself, we need to start building you up. *Build* is a really practical section, placed firmly on the foundations of *Believe*. We'll be working on your personal branding, which includes everything from how you present yourself online to your communication style and what your body language is saying. Kelly Hoppen is an expert on this: her personal brand *is* her business, so she knows just how vital this is.

Then we'll be going back to school for the only numbers lessons you ever needed: how to read a financial spreadsheet, how different business models can shape your business and the importance of sales strategies. It's vital stuff, even if you're not directly in charge of the spreadsheets. As Melanie Whelan, CEO of the cult fitness brand SoulCycle says, if you can get familiar with a P&L sheet, then that is your route to the top of the company.

Learning the nuts and bolts of any business is essential to success, but so is building up your own coping mechanisms. We discuss wellness strategies and how important they are to thrive, as Arianna Huffington has so famously spoken about. Because while it is tempting to sacrifice it all at the altar of work, and many women put themselves last in the list of priorities, it's a shortcut to ill health.

Closely linked to wellness is developing resilience to help you sustain a long career. It's such an important quality to have – and you do have to build it up – as it's crucial to getting through the knocks that life and business throw at you. We haven't met a successful woman yet who hasn't had some kind of setback along the way, from divorce or the death of a loved one to being sacked or declared bankrupt – all of these things have happened to some of the women in these pages. But it's how they deal with it that marks them out as survivors. Whitney Wolfe Herd, who founded her dating app Bumble out of the ashes of a very acrimonious split from Tinder, where she was a co-founder, has some amazing insights into the power of resilience. It's crucial reading.

Our final section is all about helping you actually become the success you want to be. In *Become* we start with a dollop of inspiration. We've profiled the most inspiring 15 women we know who have broken through their respective glass ceilings to become the first woman to do something in their company – or even country's – history. From the first woman to be president of the New York Stock Exchange (a mere 50 years after the first female trader entered the building), to the first woman to be Secretary of State to the first self-made female billionaire. They are all major firsts that will change the landscape for women coming up the ranks behind them for ever. There is no silver bullet – they've all done it in different ways – but there are some great lessons to learn from reading their stories and seeing similarities in their routes to the top.

What they all had to do on the way up – as we have – is negotiate like crazy. We all have to negotiate big and small every day, but there's a real art to getting the best deal. Whether it's a pay rise or an investment meeting there are tricks you need to learn because a negotiation is something you have to prepare, to work out in advance where you can give and take and then be ready to pivot and adapt on the day; it takes a lot of practice and we always rehearse it with each other. The language of deals is a knowledge you build up over time, and we'll give you the exact script you need when you're asking for more money. Let's also not forget that you need negotiation skills when you're navigating the world of office politics. Who better to ask for advice than a trained hostage negotiator who has saved hundreds of lives thanks to her cool-headed negotiation skills? Sue Williams has some tips that are directly transferable to your career.

Then to really propel yourself into the upper echelons you need to perfect your hustle. It's a word associated with the entrepreneurial world, but it applies just as much to those working in business, too. It's about spotting opportunities, going for them and working damn hard to turn them into success stories. Our friend, the facialist Georgia Louise, has the most incredible story about going from starting out in a rented basement treatment room to treating Linda Evangelista and a host of A-list friends. She credits her success entirely down to the hustle – and teaches you how you can harness that skill.

All these insights from the amazing women in our book are the result of us leaning on our sisterhood and encouraging them to share their wisdom. But underpinning all the tips and advice is the fact that yes, you absolutely need to work through these steps, but you need to develop your own sisterhood to do it with. How do you do that?

Well, networking is key – but it doesn't have to be in the formal way we imagine when we hear the word, which evokes starkly lit rooms and bad canapés with men in suits. There are other ways.

If you don't know other women going through the same business journey as you, it could be worth finding a group, such as the (free) AllBright Academy, which enables you to connect with other women doing exactly the same thing. Or you can build up your sisterhood from the amazing women you already know, like your oldest school friend – someone author and Professor Lynda Gratton often relies on – or a family member as the networking expert Julia Hobsbawm says she did, or a girl you met at a party, as we did.

Your sisterhood can constantly expand and change as you do, but it's crucial to your success that you build up your own bespoke network who are dedicated to empowering and improving you (and you to them). Together you have to transform the inspiration and advice in this book into actions that you do every day that will enable change. We know it, and the women in this book know it: sisterhood works. Get out there and build up yours to help you become what you want to be.

BELIEVE.

One of the things we have witnessed almost daily in our careers to date is that for many of the women we work with and meet, there is a huge gap between their actual abilities and how they perceive their capabilities. Why? We think it's due to that gnarly issue of confidence. Self-doubt, lack of self-esteem, self-deprecation, imposter syndrome – these are all real issues and they are affecting women's ability to take control of their career destinies and achieve their dreams and goals. Countless times, we've seen men overestimate their abilities and performance, while women underplay theirs. Even Madeleine Albright, the grand doyenne of American politics, has said that early on in her career she struggled to speak up in meetings.

This section is all about getting into the right frame of mind to be the boss you want to be. Whatever our visions of success are, we all have to start by looking inside ourselves and discovering what's important to us. How do we discover our personal motivations, values, goals and strengths? Can't answer that yet? Don't worry, we'll work on it together.

CHAPTER ONE

Project You

'Deep roots are not reached by the frost'

J.R.R. Tolkien

Anna

I'm the eldest of four girls, and as such, I was naturally assertive, pioneering and good at corralling people. I just assumed it would be up to me to take responsibility, to organise everyone and persuade them to follow. Taking an innate strength and turning it into a career strength for me was just a matter of perspective. I became a manager and head of department quite early in my career, as I just assumed that I should take responsibility for the activities and teams in question.

If you want to succeed in business in any industry and at any level, you've got to know yourself. According to a study by the US polling company Gallup, people who use their strengths every day are *six* times more likely to be engaged on the job, which in turn enhances the employee's productivity and career prospects and their company's bottom line. Knowing your strengths pays.

It's really important to think about your own roots and see how they might contribute to your strengths. I have found that who I am has led me down a certain career path – to the point where after many years of running businesses for others, I've ended up taking charge of my own business focused on something I feel passionate about: connecting and inspiring women. When you know what your strengths and weaknesses are, you can play with them to maximise the opportunities around you.

For many complex reasons, women are often not good at recognising and championing our strengths. It's partly to do with societal norms; we're taught as girls not to be boastful and to downplay our talents so that we get along more easily with others. But to find the confidence to champion our strengths and use them to propel our careers, we need to know what they are.

One way to figure them out is to consider the situations, tasks and relationships that give you energy, and therefore a sense of satisfaction. These are the things that keep us going when times get tough. And let's be honest, times can get tough. Very tough.

I know that I'm optimistic, a quick problem-solver and straight-talker. I have not always been super confident, though. In fact, public speaking used to fill me with terror so I had to work on that. But I have always been the first to volunteer for something that needs to be done. In my last role, as CEO of Hearst Magazines, I was used to dealing with complex business challenges and making hundreds of decisions every day. These are all qualities that have helped me work my way to the very top of a global media company, working with shareholders, huge teams of staff, clients and readers. They are qualities that I remind myself of when I have tough days.

If you need more help identifying your strengths – and weaknesses – ask around your networks. I have used an old group of friends who I started my first job with – who have now all gone on to different careers and companies, as well as former bosses, teams I've managed and now Debbie to assess my strengths and weaknesses and tell me how they think I can improve.

Having a sisterhood to help us find out more about ourselves, build up our strengths and boost us in areas where we fall short is something to develop and nurture. And, as we'll explain at the end of the book, you need a trusted panel of advisors with you throughout your career.

What you'll learn in this chapter:

- How to recognise and build up your strengths
- To celebrate the strengths of those around you
- To identify and tackle weakness
- How your sisterhood can help with 'Project You'

Recognising your strengths

It's easy to look at other business leaders and think about why we admire them: we can pick out head of the IMF Christine Lagarde's professionalism and intellect, coupled with her evident charm, or Arianna Huffington's single-minded drive and passion pared with a concern for wellbeing. Strengths are easy to identify in other people, and often those winning characteristics appear effortless.

You have your innate strengths, too. You'll know some of them, partly because they're the things that give you an energy buzz. Maybe it's something big like being able to convince anyone of anything in a sales pitch, or perhaps it's about being more detail oriented, like knowing your way around a spreadsheet. But unless you've been for a job interview lately, it's unlikely that you've sat down and thought in detail about all the strengths that make up 'Project You'.

So how do you work yours out? Here's a disarmingly simple question: can you name your three greatest strengths at work? It's an exercise Catherine Baker, founder of Sport and Beyond, a training and consulting business, often suggests as a starting point. It's not as easy as it sounds – it's often human nature, or dare we say 'female nature', to dismiss the thing that we're good at because, for us, it's easy. But it is important to consider, as it's part of recognising your personal USP and knowing what you bring to a team and workplace. So, for some, making a presentation to a roomful of strangers is no problem – like Debbie, who really shines in the limelight and gets her energy from public speaking events. For others, like me, this might be something they find more draining, preferring instead the intimacy of a one on-one-conversation where we are likely to excel. That's not to say you can't learn other skills, or that you have to avoid certain situations, but it's helpful to think where your talents naturally lie.

Sahar Hashemi, OBE, has an important lesson on finding your strengths. She was working in a big law firm where she gradually realised that, actually, she wasn't very good. 'While other people around me were shining,

I was mediocre; the job didn't play to my strengths,' she says. She quit and co-founded the coffee bar chain Coffee Republic in 1995 (more on her inspirational story coming up in chapter four). 'If you feel you're not in sync and not enjoying the work that you're doing, you need to look for something that you love that plays to your strengths,' she adds. 'Success means finding something that you shine in; everyone can be a star in their own area. I wish I'd told my 20-something self that you'll find something you'll love and you're good at. Don't stop till you find that.' It's such an important lesson to learn; you can find what you're good at at any age.

Ask around

But working out your strengths really doesn't have to be a solo project: tap into your sisterhood because they might suggest things that surprise you. Former and current work colleagues will know exactly what you're good at – they see you every day. It's so important to have a diverse sisterhood, with different work experiences and different outlooks, because it can offer a different perspective. For example, while Debbie has been an entrepreneur all her business life, so sometimes we have very different skills and outlooks that complement each other. Look around at the people in your sisterhood and ask whether there is a diverse range of experience. If there's not, try to add that in.

Also, don't be afraid to ask your boss – after all, it is in their interest to have the best employee they can. If you have a good relationship with your boss, and they want to see you succeed, they can definitely be part of your sisterhood. It was my boss who highlighted my talent for inspiring people to follow me – something I probably knew deep down, but hadn't recognised as a core strength. This was crucial later when I was CEO of a company that was undergoing a merger, diversifying, incorporating a new culture and working out where it could make savings – I really had to bring the whole company along with me if it was going to work.

How to build on your strengths

Once you've identified your strengths, it's time to extract those golden nuggets, build them up, flex them and use them as often as you can. List your three greatest strengths and ask yourself if you're using them as often as possible, perhaps by identifying how many hours a day or week you use them, and how can you employ them more often. Your strengths are like little muscles that need to be exercised daily.

Build up others

It would be hard to find a better example of a woman who knows her personal strengths inside out than an Olympic-gold-winning athlete. Crista Cullen MBE won gold for GB in the 2016 Rio Olympic Games in hockey – all the while balancing training with her day job. She even heroically came back on the field after getting her head stitched up part way through a match. She says that it wouldn't have been possible without knowing her – and her teammates' – strengths inside out: 'We won an Olympic gold because of what we did off the field – investing in the people in our team,' she says. 'We were really good at drawing out each other's strengths, and really understanding each other.'

It may be the secret for success in winning an Olympic gold, but it's directly translatable to business, too. If you're a leader at any level you can get more out of your team by working through this chapter with them too. Research by the UK's Corporate Leadership Council found that when managers focus on the strength of an employee their performance improves by 36 per cent; when they criticise them their performance dips by 27 per cent. Not only is it crucial to the idea of a sisterhood to nurture and develop those around us, but it translates to greater success for your team: Gallup data shows that teams that focus on strengths every day are 12.5 per cent more productive.

As your sisterhood is another team, consider doing the same exercise with them, too. By helping identify their own strengths, you'll be supporting and enhancing their careers.

Identifying weakness

We've identified our strengths, but we can't ignore our weaknesses in the bigger picture of 'Project You'. We might be aware of, or at least be better at articulating our shortcomings more than our strengths, but there will still be some blind spots. Just as you asked for help identifying your positives, don't be afraid to crowd source your weaknesses too, as I did when I asked my former team for feedback.

Joanna Coles OBE, who is now an executive producer, but has also held the roles of chief content officer for Hearst and former editor-in-chief of *Cosmopolitan* US, has this advice: 'The best feedback you can have is really listening to and watching how people respond to you and being honest about it. The Chanel guru Karl Lagerfeld always said he never needed a shrink because he asked himself tough questions every day. I try to do this – though it's really difficult. I think feedback depends a lot upon the person who is giving it to you and whether you respect them and trust their motives. But if you are in a customer-based business, the best feedback of all is the numbers. Nothing speaks louder.'

Perhaps it's that you don't have enough confidence in your talents and so aren't decisive enough. Or maybe you don't delegate enough, because you want a job done a certain way, but that means you struggle to hit deadlines. Katy Koob, vice president of Refinery29, says she's struggled with this: 'I get excited about everything and it's been one of my biggest self-realisations – that I have to learn to say no in order to keep growing.'

When I left my last role, I asked for feedback from my team – you can glean invaluable insight about yourself from those that you manage, as well as those higher up the corporate ladder. They said that I was not very good at celebrating success. I'm now actively trying to stop to take a bit of time to look backwards too, and to celebrate the wins. Don't be afraid to ask people for a critique, and don't let them get away with just praising you. Tell them that you need their honest assessment in order to grow – and that you can offer the same service back.

Strengths that become weaknesses

There is a tipping point to strengths; sometimes if they are too strong, they become weaknesses. Debbie and I are very similar in the way we run full tilt at everything: we move very fast and make quick decisions. This means we can achieve a lot – things that can perhaps look daunting to those on the outside – but we're very aware that working in this way could easily become a weakness. While we're speeding forwards, our team sometimes struggles to keep up. It's challenging to keep people motivated and focused if you're constantly moving at a fast pace. Sometimes we need to remind each other to keep everyone else on board.

Research shows that people are more likely to fail when their strengths are used in the wrong way, at the wrong time or in the wrong situations. For example, those of us who are good at making decisions quickly (note to ourselves) can fail because we don't collaborate enough. Others who are famed for their perfectionism can miss deadlines, be poor delegators and misjudge effort versus output. For those of us who are leaders and bosses, it's important to be aware of areas where we might be pushing in the wrong direction.

Accepting some weakness

Once you've identified your weaknesses, you don't always need to dwell on them. Some shortcomings are OK; they are part of life and part of business. 'One piece of advice I would give to myself in my younger years is that it's OK to make mistakes – that's how you get to the right answer,' says

Michelle Kennedy, whose business experience spans being a corporate lawyer, the deputy COO of Badoo, the world's largest dating platform, and now an entrepreneur. 'Maybe I would have saved myself a few years of beating myself up if someone had told me that at the start.'

Sometimes we just have to learn how to do something to an acceptable performance level rather than aiming for perfection in order to get the job done on time. Debbie and I have a similar philosophy in that we feel that if we get it right eight or nine times out of ten, then we're doing well. Perfection sometimes has to be sacrificed for getting the job done.

Just as not all of our weaknesses need to be fixed, some can be delegated. As founders and leaders – particularly new ones – it can be really tempting to want to manage everything ourselves. But it's just not possible; as your business expands, or you move up the ranks in a corporation, your capacity to do absolutely everything necessarily dwindles.

Work on them together

An important piece of research undertaken by the leadership consultancy company Zenger Folkman found that although tackling a weakness on its own does improve leaders, those who work on a combination of strengths and weaknesses improved nearly three times as much. Don't try to merely 'fix' all your weaknesses; instead concentrate on strengths you can build up at the same time. Building up your strengths and weaknesses is a personal cocktail that takes a lifetime of work, so keep coming back to this chapter, and work on 'Project You' with your sisterhood.

CASE STUDY: NAOMIE HARRIS OBE, HOLLYWOOD ACTRESS

Naomie Harris is an award-winning actress whose power-ful, leading roles have included Winnie Mandela in 2013's *Mandela: Long Walk to Freedom* and the updated Eve Moneypenny in the Bond films *Skyfall* and *Spectre*, where she famously asked for press material to refer to her as a 'Bond woman', rather than the traditional 'Bond girl'. She is a founder member of our first AllBright club in London.

Naomie's job necessarily entails digging deep into her personal character in order to mine it for the roles she plays, so she's hyper-aware of her own personal strengths and weaknesses. She thinks that knowing them is crucial for us all. 'Understanding how your strengths can both help and hinder you is a really important part of understanding your-self and how to maximise your effectiveness in life,' Naomie confirms. 'One of my greatest strengths as an actress is my sensitivity, while another of my strengths is my honesty and desire to find "the truth".'

She has been working since the age of nine and has learned the strength to not take rejection personally (a very hard lesson for many of us, whatever our profession). 'There aren't any actors who get every role they go up for,' she says. 'My way of dealing with that rejection has been to make a mental separation between what is a rejection of me personally and what is a rejection of my interpreta-tion of a character. Someone who auditions me for 10–20 minutes doesn't know anything about me, they only know my interpretation of a role, so it really doesn't make sense for me to take the rejection personally, and if the rejection isn't personal then I find it much easier to shrug off.'

But, she says, 'The reality is that every strength can tip over into a weakness. Being sensitive is a real hindrance in everyday life.' She explains that while her honesty and quest for the truth, 'is a brilliant part of the arsenal of being an actress, it can cause a lot of conflict in personal relationships; as not everyone wants an open, honest conversation.'

Her final takeaway is especially useful: 'I think one of my greatest acquired strengths has been learning to navigate when and how my strengths become weaknesses in certain contexts and vice versa in other situations, and using them appropriately.' It's a tough act to pull off – but is a lesson that applies just as much to business as to acting.

CHAPTER RECAP: Project You

You've made it through the first chapter, and there's been a lot of advice to absorb. Here's a digested read that you can refer back to. We recommend working through this summary and the worksheet with someone from your work sisterhood who wants to empower and improve herself, too.

Recognising strengths: Try thinking about what gives you energy and what you enjoy. If you need help, ask around in your work sisterhood, and make time for sessions with your boss who could be crucial in your strength-building success. This is an important first step in 'Project You'.

Building strengths: Make sure that you are using your strengths as much as possible at work; if you're not, then you might be on the wrong career path. It's equally important to build up those around you, too. It's crucial to your success as a team leader. Meanwhile, watch out for strengths that, left unchecked, can tip over and become weaknesses.

Identifying and tackling weakness: Accept that we all have weaknesses, it's what makes us human and they are a vital part of 'Project You'. Once you know what your weaknesses are – and again, ask for help identifying them if you need it – some can be parked or delegated out, while others need to be addressed. Do this in conjunction with your strength-building work for the best possible success outcomes.

WORKSHEET: HOW TO IDENTIFY AND OPTIMISE YOUR STRENGTHS

IDENTIFYING STRENGTHS:

To identify your strengths, reflect on the following questions:

1. What things do you do well? What comes easily to you?

_____

_____

_____

_____

2. What activities make you feel excited and energised (as opposed to drained)?

_____

_____

_____

_____

3. Consider feedback you have received for tasks done well. What was the task?

_____

_____

_____

_____

DEVELOPING YOUR STRENGTHS:

Imagine you were able to spend more of your time doing the things you like to do and are good at. While that may not be feasible 100 per cent of the time, there's no reason why we can't strive for a better balance.

Take a moment to ask yourself:

1. What strengths do I use less often?

_____

_____

_____

_____

2. What on-the-job experiences (project work, stretch assignments, team roles, etc.) will help stretch and maximise these strengths?

_____

_____

_____

_____

3. Who can coach, mentor and provide feedback to help me develop my areas of strength?

_____

_____

_____

_____

CHAPTER TWO

Drive and Motivation

'Our goals can only be reached through a vehicle of a plan, in which we must fervently believe, and upon which we must vigorously act. There is no other route to success'

Pablo Picasso

Debbie

Every New Year's Eve I take out the same old notebook and write my goals for the year, both personal and business. I've found that when I write things down they're more likely to get done, so I think that this process is key to my success. Research backs this up: a recent study by Dominican University found that those who set goals were 33 per cent more successful than those who didn't, while those who made themselves accountable – for example by emailing a weekly progress report to a friend – accomplished even more. I look at my notebook halfway through the year and see that I'm on track. If I'm not, I check that it's still a priority and use it as motivation to get cracking. Obviously I do better in some years than in others.

We're used to hearing about motivation and goals from incredible sportswomen. Serena Williams started the hashtag

#WhatIsYourS, challenging her fans to come up with an 'S' word that means something to them, that inspires and motivates them. She said hers were strength and sureness – her specific qualities which are immediately recognisable to any tennis fan.

It's no different when it comes to your career. To be successful and push yourself forward you need to think about your motivations. For me, entrepreneurship was what I grew up with. My grandmother and mother would not have described themselves as entrepreneurs, but with a chain of sweetshops/off licences and a printing company, that is what they were. We discussed business around the kitchen table, and it normalised this for me as a child. I simply didn't have anyone in my immediate family who had a 'normal job', i.e. who was employed by someone else. So one of my first long-term goals was to work for myself. My siblings also work for themselves – so something obviously rubbed off.

I've always been very driven. I wanted to be the best at whatever I was going to try to do. I don't really compare myself to others, but I am very motivated by what I've already achieved. For me, the next project or business always has to be bigger than the last one – I'm into empire building. Now, my goal is to bring about change in the number of women who lead businesses. That is a long-term one, but I've got lots of short-term ones to help me get there.

Forget that oft-quoted cheesy business adage that if you find what you love, you'll never work a day in your life. It's nonsense. If you find what you love, in our experience, you'll work harder than ever before because you'll have found your calling, your source of energy.

Many of us are now seeking out a business career that is rooted in a wider sense of purpose and an active desire to do good in the world. We have done this with our own company, AllBright, which aims to inspire change by championing, connecting and upskilling women to achieve their career ambitions. As Arianna Huffington says in *Thrive*, 'Making money and doing good in the world are not mutually exclusive.' Purpose with profit is a business trend really making waves at the moment, with many brands connecting with a deeper social enterprise. We've found that creating something that has a wide social impact really increases your motivation to make the business work – especially when we see the visible effect it has on our members.

While new research suggests that Generation Z – those aged 18–25 – are more motivated by job satisfaction than by money, cash is still a driving force for a lot of our members: 36 per cent would like to make a significant profit and 34 per cent would like to eventually sell their businesses for a profit or go public. It is for me, too, because in my world of building businesses, there's a direct correlation between money and success. It's not something to be shy about: financial independence is so important for women, and not something we talk about often enough, but it should be a key motivation for us all. It became mine when I was newly divorced and building Love Home Swap. I had a very real obligation to make sure I could provide money for my children. I can't tell you how motivating that was.

Thinking about what you want out of life is an ongoing process. It's totally normal that your motivations change over time as you build up experience and develop relationships around you. Anna, for instance, got to the top of her career as CEO and then realised that her motivations and goals had shifted: she wanted freedom, pace and the opportunity to build something from scratch. She says it's harder, with longer hours, but more rewarding; now she never dreads coming to work. Which is what we want for you – and it starts here with working out your motivations and writing down your goals.

What you'll learn in this chapter:

- To understand your personal values and motivations
- The importance of goals and how to set them
- How to hold yourself to account

Values versus motivations

Your values are very different from your motivations. Values are guiding, overarching principles; generally things we've been brought up to believe in and what we look for in other people – be that friends, romantic partners, colleagues and even organisations that we work for. While you can choose them, they might feel more fixed in your core belief system.

After leaving Tinder, which she co-founded in 2012, Whitney Wolfe Herd experienced online bullying in the storm of her departure. In the light of this experience, she decided that values of kindness, equality and confidence were of crucial importance to her next business venture, and the online world that she wanted to create. Now they are at the heart of Bumble. For us, our values are centred around helping other women achieve success, which is at the core of our own business. Your values can shape your career.

Understanding motivations

Motivations are what make you leap out of bed – even before 5.30am, as I do (I'm a fiendishly early riser, but I realise that isn't for everyone!). As Thomasina Miers, founder of the popular UK high street restaurant chain Wahaca says, 'Life can be tough, but if what you're doing makes you feel fulfilled, you find yourself being a happier person. Not waking up instantly grinning, of course, but experiencing a more grounded, "I know what I'm doing today" kind of satisfaction.'

It's hard to put your own motivations down on paper, so it takes some soul-searching. I wanted to work for myself, I love having new projects on the go, I find building businesses energising. Some of these motivations you only discover over time. Whatever your motivations are, make no mistake that as soon as you become a business owner or rise up through the ranks of a corporation, there's an awful lot of grit and determination that goes into it, every day.

Why do we go to work?

Thinking about why you leave the house to go to work in the morning is a good start when figuring this out. Are you doing a job to pay the bills? Is it a career in which you want to climb the ladder? Or is it a passion that will leave a legacy? Or (typically) some combination of the three? Money will often be a motivator – you have to feed yourself and your family, plus it is also a fundamental marker of success. Indeed, in the entrepreneurial world, if you're not making money for your shareholders and yourself, then you're not doing your job. As Sara Blakely, founder and billionaire entrepreneur behind Spanx, said, 'I've never subscribed to the idea that money's bad or that I shouldn't have a lot of it, because I think it's great. I think it's fun to make, fun to spend and fun to give away.'

Similarly, if status and being the most senior person in the organisation is important to you, then don't be apologetic about that either. 'The more honest you can be the more likely you will be to create a plan that matters to you,' says executive coach Helen Hatton. You might have to keep up this conversation with yourself as you change and evolve.

Finding your passion

Thomasina Miers struggled to find her way for 10 years in a series of jobs that weren't quite right, until she realised that a deep-rooted love of food was her true passion. 'When I left school, a career in food wasn't really seen as a viable option. I spent about a decade trying to find a career that fitted. But I realised that I think about food all day long, from what I'm going to have for breakfast to what I'm going to cook some girlfriends for supper. I just wanted to do something I loved.' So, if there's something that you find yourself talking and thinking about over and over again, that's probably a key motivation.

If it's not as obvious as Thomasina's, it can seem bewildering to try to pin your passion down. There is, after all, so much choice available to us now, with jobs such as 'influencer' and 'coders' that weren't even dreamt up when most of us took career advice at school. If this is you, we suggest you start by asking the members of your sisterhood what *they* think is important to you. People who care about you can often see things more clearly from the outside.

It was a woman in Michelle Kennedy's sisterhood who prompted her to launch her app connecting mothers in their local area. 'I was moaning about the fact that, as a new mother, I had no mum friends locally and that there wasn't an app that acted like a dating app. Eventually, after I'd gone on about it for ages, my best mate said, "Can you just do this? I'm sick of hearing about it."' So, she did. Her friend gave her the kick she needed.

Setting goals

Once you've discovered your motivations, you can use them to set your personal goals. 'I constantly set goals and really try to think about where I want to be. I don't believe we should ever be stagnant, so I always push myself to try new things. I like having goals to strive for,' Katy Koob, vice president of Refinery29, says.

The most successful people in business often credit their ability to turn ambition into results by having clear goals written down (as you know, I'm one of them). Emma Stone decided that she desperately wanted to be an actress at the age of 14. She made a PowerPoint presentation entitled

'Project Hollywood' and crafted a pitch deck about why she needed to move from her home in Arizona to California, be home-schooled and attend auditions. Amazingly, her parents saw merit in her plan. ('It's nuts that they agreed to it,' Emma said recently.) But perhaps they saw the clear passion in their now Oscar-winning daughter's goal and believed in her steely vision.

Goals can also provide motivation to doggedly stick at a path even if the going gets tough – and we'll go through why building up resilience is essential to success in chapter eight.

How to set your goals

The author Neil Gaiman, whose novels include *Stardust, American Gods* and *Coraline*, said in a 2012 commencement speech at the University of the Arts that when he was 15, he wrote a list of everything he wanted to do in his life. 'I didn't have a career, I just did everything on that list.' You need a list of your own.

In order to make sure you're setting the right targets, you need space and time to think. 'Really try to disconnect from the laptop, your phone, your desk,' executive coach Nicola Porter advises. 'If you can get moving, get outside, lie in the park, go for a run. Do whatever you need to do to disentangle from daily life. Give yourself permission to think big, about your life, your career, about your business. This is brainstorming and there are no wrong ideas in a brainstorm. Be bold, be creative, be ambitious. Don't put any parameters or any limits around yourself.' How ambitious should you be? Nicola says if one is easy and ten is nearly impossible, you should be aiming for a nine.

The kinds of questions you should be asking yourself are:

- What would I love to achieve?
- What do I really care about?
- What's important to me?
- What's my purpose?
- What do I want to be known for?
- If fear or money or time wasn't a factor, what would I long to do?

The next step is to share these with someone in your sisterhood to help keep you accountable.

Short- and long-term goals

It's not enough to have one list of goals. 'If you want to get ahead in life, you need to have a three-year, five-year, ten-year plan in place,' Farrah Storr, the UK editor of *Cosmopolitan*, advises. 'Because without that you're not going to push yourself to get there. So, make sure you have that – and write it down. It will be a beacon at the end for those times when you hit the roadblocks which are always on the road to success.'

After university, I briefly worked for a management consultancy company; it was enough time to learn that I wanted to work for myself – that was my big long-term goal. Now my – and Anna's – long-term goal is to increase the number of women in the boardroom and grow the amount of venture capital being invested in female-led business. But we need baby steps to get there, so our short-term goals have been things like setting up the online AllBright Academy, which we hope will become a global community for women to connect and support one another, and to write a book sharing advice gleaned from our years of experience. Our short-term goals have been achieved and we constantly set more. The long-term goal, well, that's a work in progress, and it involves you!

CASE STUDY: ANASTASIA SOARE, CEO AND FOUNDER OF ANASTASIA BEVERLY HILLS

When Anastasia Soare left her native Romania, she knew that her motivation was 'to be significant', she says. 'I wanted to prove to myself that I was capable of doing many things. I wanted to have a purpose, to wake up in the morning and do something that will improve other people's lives.' Her motivation was also, she readily admits, to provide for her daughter. 'I was a single mom who needed to make a living.'

She has achieved all those ambitions, and more. Known as the 'Eyebrow Queen', as CEO and founder of Anastasia Beverly Hills, she is one of America's self-made female billionaires. But she says the road to the top has been hard – and one she couldn't have travelled without sticking to her motivations and vision.

Anastasia left her native Romania 30 years ago and moved to the US with her young daughter, not speaking a word of English. She had trained at architectural college, 'But I knew that without speaking the language I would not be able to get a job in my profession. So, I went to beauty school, and after a few months I started working as an aesthetician.' Here her two disciplines combined. Having studied art and archi-tecture, including the golden ratio theory and Leonardo da Vinci's studies on the human body, she knew about balance and proportion – specifically in facial features. 'I started going to the library and developing a technique on how to shape the eyebrow according to the golden ratio theory,' she says.

While it was common in Romania to get a facial followed by an eyebrow shape, it wasn't the norm in the USA in 1989. 'I was quite surprised,' she says. 'I was giving facials to some of the most important celebrities in Hollywood and nobody paid attention to eyebrows.' She spotted a huge business opportunity.

Although others didn't always see it: her first landlord wasn't keen to rent her a room, 'because he thought that I would not be able to pay the rent doing eyebrows'. But her clients – who included Claudia Schiffer and Naomi Campbell from the early days – believed in her. From there, busi-ness boomed: women waited as long as three hours to see Anastasia. The work was long and hard: Anastasia worked from 9am to 10pm, as well as travelling around the country at weekends to promote her business. 'The only time when I didn't work was when I slept,' she says.

Her popularity only increased when Oprah gave her the seal of approval, and later, Michelle Obama, when she invited her to the White House. 'That was when I thought, "I've made it".' She really has.

CHAPTER RECAP: Motivations And Goals

Your motivations and goals are part of the foundations of 'Project You' and they're worth spending time thinking about to drive your career down the path you want it to go.

Values vs motivations: When you're working out what drives you, it's useful to think of the difference between values and motivations, which both inform your business personality, and both are important to stick to if you want to succeed.

Passion: There's also sometimes the big driving passion that can give you real fire in your belly. If you can identify that, you can shape a meaningful career around it. Not everyone has this; you're lucky if you do.

Importance of goals: Research consistently shows that setting goals – and writing them down – is crucial to success. You'll need long- and short-term goals.

How to set goals: Give yourself time and space to think. Then write down a series of goals. Put a time frame on them and think about *how* you can achieve them. Then make yourself accountable: tap into your work sisterhood and share your goals.

WORKSHEET: SETTING YOUR GOALS

The first part of your task is to dream big. Ask yourself a series of big questions: what would you want to be known for? If money and time weren't factors, what would you like to be? Then you need to set this down in writing in the form of goals – what do you need to do to become that person? As you do, think about your reactions as you answer these questions. What are you getting excited about? The next step is to share your answers with someone in your business sisterhood to hold you accountable.

GOAL-SETTING PART 1:

What do I want to achieve?

a. In the next six weeks:

_____

_____

_____

_____

b. In the next six months:

_____

_____

_____

_____

c. In the next year:

_____

_____

_____

_____

d. In the next five years:

_____

_____

_____

_____

GOAL-SETTING PART 2:

Once you've identified your goals you must think about the practical steps you need to take to make your goals a reality. Below is a framework using a commonly used goal-setting system known as SMART, which will help you set clear objectives. You can repeat this process for each goal you want to focus on.

Specific (What do I want to accomplish? Why is this goal important?):

_____

_____

_____

_____

Measurable (How will I know when this goal is accomplished?):

_____

_____

_____

_____

Achievable (How do I accomplish this goal? What are the
constraints I need to consider?):

_____

_____

_____

_____

Relevant (Does this goal match my wider objectives? Is the
timing right?):

_____

_____

_____

_____

Timely (What can I do today to achieve this? What can I have
achieved in six weeks' time? In six months?):

_____

_____

_____

_____

CHAPTER THREE

The 10-step Confidence Plan

'Women don't need to find their voice, they need to be empowered to use it and people need to be urged to listen'

Duchess of Sussex

Anna

I can still picture the most terrifying moment of my career. I was the newly appointed COO of Hearst and my boss wanted to call an all-company meeting for 1,000 employees. He said we'd hold it in the Odeon cinema in Leicester Square, in the vast screening space where all the big film premieres are held. The most public speaking I'd done at this point was in front of a table of 15 people. The stakes were high; I knew that if I didn't nail it, I would lose everyone's respect as a new leader, so I was absolutely terrified. I decided the only way to approach this was with total preparation – everything scripted and rehearsed, from what I was going to say to the way I was going to stand. When the spotlight was on me and I looked out on a sea of 1,000 faces, thanks to my preparation, I knew I could pull it off. It was like jumping off the high board, and even though I've been in challenging situations since, nothing has been as terrifying.

Confidence is a complex thing; it ebbs and flows over a lifetime and it's hard to pinpoint why. The truth is that lots of people are nervous. What about if you had the talent, brains and looks of a Hollywood actress like Naomie Harris? You'd never be underconfident, right? Wrong. 'I have crises of confidence all the time,' she says. 'One of the greatest life lessons I've learned is that EVERYONE has them all the time too! Before every single role I've ever played I think I can't find the character, and after every job I think I've done it awfully and will be discovered as a terrible actress. It was such a relief to learn from speaking to other actors in the industry that I hugely admire, like Kate Winslet and Judi Dench, that they have exactly the same fears.' It's not just actors; believe me when I say that if you look at any seemingly confident, pulled-together woman, there have been times when she's been quietly panicking.

Boosting women's confidence in themselves and their business ideas is the greatest challenge to closing the pay gap, promoting more female executives and encouraging female entrepreneurs. According to the recent Facebook campaign #SheMeansBusiness, 25 per cent of women said that a lack of confidence was stopping them starting their own business, which as a female entrepreneur and investor myself is so disheartening to hear.

Female confidence is tricky. There are cultural norms at work that mean many societies' expectation of women is that they are polite and modest, and there are many structural things we need to do with the business landscape to help address these factors. But there are also tweaks we can make to our own behaviours, too.

It's essential that we project confidence if we want to advance our careers. Debbie and I have both noticed that in general men are more confident than women in business meetings. Not always, of course, but often. It's backed up by statistics: men tend to overestimate their abilities by around 30 per cent, according to Columbia Business School in New York. The research claims they are not faking it; they genuinely believe it. Added to this, studies show that men are often hired and promoted based on their potential, while for women it's based on what they've already achieved, with the obvious result that more men reach the top more quickly. 'I think there is pretty good behavioural science that has proven the idea that, essentially if men think they have 5–6 of the 10 skills needed for a next level they are inclined to say "bring it!" while if women have 9 of the 10 they are more inclined to say "I'm not sure if I'm fully qualified",' Marisa Thalberg, CMO of Taco Bell Corp says. 'Just knowing that has been helpful to me.'

Meanwhile, as women, we can sometimes betray our lack of confidence in small unknowing gestures. I once had an extremely skilled senior woman on my team who suffered from low self-esteem. She would bluster into important meetings late, find a seat at the back of the room (instead of next to me, where she should have been as one of my right-hand people). She came across as distracted and defensive when she made her points and her colleagues often gave her a hard time. I found this extremely frustrating, as she was one of our most talented team members. We worked on some tweaks to help her feel more confident. Firstly, preparation: thinking about what she wanted to get out of the meeting beforehand and talking to me about the agenda and her part in the meeting. Secondly, playing the part and being professional: arriving in good time, sitting next to me, projecting confidence, focusing on the content of the meeting and presenting her arguments in a clear and compelling way. These were small adjustments, but they worked very well and after a few meetings the turnaround was astonishing. Her self-confidence grew by the week and before long her imposter syndrome had abated and she was promoted to a more senior role.

We all need to be aware of the small gestures and habits that can have a huge subliminal impact. If you're not naturally confident in a certain situation, you need to draw on your reserves, and this is where the ground work in chapters one and two come in. You need to have a deep understanding of your strengths and your goals in order to remind yourself why you're in the position you are and where you want to be. You've got to be the best, and that starts with believing you are.

Your 10-step confidence plan

1. Be prepared

If you met Kathryn Parsons, CEO of Decoded, a business that teaches companies and governments on how to embrace technology, from AI to blockchain, in more than 85 cities around the world, you would not imagine her to be lacking in confidence. She's smart, articulate and full of passion for her brand and the future of women entrepreneurs. And yet, she says, 'I was so nervous at the start I used to pass out on stage, I'm not joking.' What did she do about it? She turned her fear of public speaking into an academic exercise that she had to crack, reading books on confidence, how to speak and how to own her space. She says that, eventually, 'I learned to pitch my story and be brave.'

Similarly, Susan Cain, the author of the wildly popular book *Quiet*, which is about the power of the introvert personality, says she spent a year practising her TED talk on the subject, because as a natural introvert she was terrified. It paid off – she totally nailed it and her seemingly effortless speech has now had more than 20 million views.

When people look comfortable, it's usually because they're prepared. For my all-company presentation I saw a public speaking expert to help me with how to hold myself and voice projection; I also learned my script by rote and practised, practised, practised until I was sure I could deliver it even if I were overcome with nerves on the day. I pulled it off – but it's important to show that it was with the help of an extended network of professionals and sisterhood who I practised on.

Preparation is important whether you're addressing an auditorium, presenting a sales pitch or brainstorming with your boss. Make sure you know what you want to say – even if you need having bullet points written down on a cue card. We are judged in seconds from when we walk into a room, so think about what you wear – it has to be something that makes you feel comfortable and confident, while being appropriate for the level of meeting. Decide where you will sit, and make sure you know who else will be there (cribbing up on them where necessary). These are all things that can be prepared in advance and they're the first step in your confidence plan.

2. Own your space

Women can have a tendency to physically shrink and be apologetic. Big meetings can sometimes feel overwhelming, but you've got to rise up and be physically confident – something both Debbie and I have learned to master over the years. It's really important, especially if you're the only woman in the room, to return that handshake firmly, to hold that stare and maintain eye contact.

How do you use your body to take up all of your space in an authentic way that conveys authority, confidence and credibility (but without it looking too obviously like a power stance)? Abi Eniola, a communications tutor at RADA Business, says, 'Stand with your legs hip width apart, feet parallel; really feel the ground with your feet and adjust yourself so weight is easily distributed. Soften your knees, imagine your shoulders are floating open and your head pulling upwards from the back of your skull.' It's about owning the physical space around you, and not letting yourself be cowed. Harvard Business School professor Amy Cuddy's famous TED talk on body language revealed that by assuming the position of someone more confident, we can essentially trick our brains to give us a confidence boost – as well as projecting that out to others.

Nicola Mendelsohn, Facebook vice president for Europe, Middle East and Africa, warns that owning your space extends to stopping yourself doing things that you might find yourself doing without thinking about it: like pouring the drinks in a meeting. 'Do not pour the coffee or do any of the housekeeping things that women traditionally do,' she says. The act of performing 'mother' in a meeting can tap into the unconscious bias of those around you and diminish your value in their eyes.

3. Use your voice

Far too often women don't say anything in meetings. It's something Debbie and I have witnessed among women in many forums, and it's so frustrating. It happens to even the most confident of us, as Nicola recalls. 'When I was younger, at the start of my career, I would sit in meetings and would know the answer to a question but wait for someone else to say something. When they did, I would kick myself for not having spoken up. Every time I did find the confidence to say something, it was usually the right thing to do. I had to tell myself I have a right to speak, I'm being paid to do this.'

It's not a trait exclusive to juniors – women of all ages and stages in their careers can be guilty of not speaking up. Plucking up the confidence to speak is something that gets easier with practice. Try speaking at the start of a meeting to get your point in early and make a confident start. Nicola says a bugbear of hers is that often women start by apologising. 'They start with, "can I just say" or "I'm sorry but ..." and I think, "No! You're here for your opinion," so speak your mind and be confident.'

It's those little comments we can all find ourselves making, such as 'correct me if I'm wrong' or 'I know I'm not the expert on this ...', which have been dubbed 'out-of-power' language. When Professor Judith Baxter from Aston University studied the language of senior executives, she found that women used these terms *four times* as often as men. We do ourselves down before anyone else has the chance to.

Nicola Mendelsohn adds that if you find someone speaking over you – as she says she sees men often doing to women in meetings (and we've seen too) – make sure you win that conversation back. If it happens to another woman in your meeting, help out by saying something like, 'I'd love to return to XX's point before she was cut off ...' It makes a point, politely, that women deserve to be heard.

Debbie and I are good at presenting, now. But this confidence has been hard won through practice – we've had to speak at countless investor, shareholder and company meetings, as well as public speaking engagements and to media. Every woman, no matter how successful she is, still has moments where that bravado slips – even Oprah has admitted that, despite being a veteran broadcaster, during her famous 2018 Golden Globes speech she was 'more nervous than I thought, because I've never had a dry mouth before. In the middle of the speech I thought, "I can't move my gums".'

Farrah Storr, who is also the author of the book *The Discomfort Zone*, has this comforting advice for weathering those moments and forcing yourself to speak up: 'Discomfort is not one huge monolithic experience, it's only brief moments. Whether it's public speaking or speaking in front of your boss, you have to have a plan for that moment when you walk on stage, or what you start by saying. Once you have a plan for those key moments of discomfort, the moments in between are as easy as breathing.'

Maryam Pasha, a speaking coach and director of TEDxLondon, says her pet peeve 'is when people get up on stage and start apologising – "can you hear me at the back? I'm sorry, my voice isn't strong." I always tell people to have their first and last paragraph memorised – have your runway so you've got your take-off and landing smoothly. You've got to start strong and end strong.'

4. Take a deep breath

Speaking of breathing, you can tell if someone is nervous if they're taking short, shallow breaths. Amisha Ghadiali, who, after working in politics for a congressman in the US and an MP in Westminster, is now a wellbeing mentor, recommends this breathing technique before a big meeting – or even just when you open your laptop to start a project. 'Taking a deep breath, right into the belly so the whole belly and chest fills with air, connects to your solar plexus in the stomach, which is a place of personal power from an energy perspective.' At the same time as taking your deep breaths, you should visualise what you want to get out of the upcoming meeting. 'By connecting to your intention as you breathe, it helps tune you into your priority,' she says.

It's actually a simple – and very easy to implement – form of meditation, something many CEOs and business leaders such as Arianna Huffington say they practise. Over time, meditation strengthens the area of the brain called the amygdala, which is responsible for our fear, or fight or flight response. The more you practise, the less scared you will become in stressful situations.

5. Connect to your audience

If you're nervous about speaking, be it in a one-on-one meeting with a superior, or a public speaking engagement, Maryam suggests you, 'Ask yourself this very simple question:

why am I speaking?' By doing this you will hopefully identify your core message, and focus on that higher purpose, rather than your nerves.

The next question is, *who* is your audience? 'It means thinking about what they care about, what their priorities are and why they are listening to you. You need the audience to give you permission to go into their mind and plant an idea,' Maryam says. It's a really powerful tactic, and one that often gets forgotten. If you can connect with the person or people you're speaking with, you'll have them eating out of the palm of your hand.

6. Banish imposter syndrome

Guess what? Almost everyone battles feelings that they're not good enough, and that at any moment they're going to be found out, whatever level of seniority they are at. Even the impressive Whitney Wolfe Herd admits, 'Just because I'm the CEO of a company, it doesn't mean I don't get nervous.'

If you are doubting yourself, 'I really encourage you to break the silence and tell someone else,' Maryam Pasha says. 'I know that's a scary thought because part of the problem is that you're afraid of being found out.' She says that she's found that once she has confessed to someone, it very often gets reciprocated. 'Even from people that I thought had endless amounts of confidence.'

How do we believe in ourselves? 'The key is to hear the fearful voice in your head that knocks your confidence and DON'T ignore it or try to get rid of it,' actress Naomie Harris says. 'Instead listen with compassion. Recognise that the fear and lack of confidence come from the part of you that needs reassurance and give yourself that reassurance in a way that you know works for you. I like to talk to the fearful part of me like a child; I say things like, "I know this role seems insurmountable, which is why you're telling me I'm not good enough, but we've been here many times before and we've got through this and gone on to produce great work, so don't worry I've got this, you don't have to be scared." That kind of soothing self-talk works wonders for me.'

7. Tackle the motherhood gap

Debbie and I both have two children, and countless working friends do too. High-profile businesswomen manage with large families, including Dame Helena Morrissey, head of personal investing at Legal & General, who famously has nine children, while Susan Wojcicki, the CEO of YouTube, has five.

But I know from personal experience there are inevitably huge issues of confidence that arise when you return to work after maternity leave, or any leave of absence. The thing you have to remember is that your career is the muscle you've used for way longer than your parenting muscle. You might think that everything has changed – and it has in your world – but probably very little has been quite as seismic at work.

Some of the best companies are getting much better at helping women return to work, but there's lots you can do to help yourself, too.

To start with, if you take a longer maternity leave period – something that's perhaps not an option in the USA or if you own your own company – then you can use it as a chance to upskill. Go to a talk (we've had lots of talks at The AllBright where women have brought babies along too), start a blog or podcast, sign up for an e-learning course and go back to work feeling more confident.

Secondly, stay connected while you're off. That doesn't mean working, just keeping up with what's going on and staying in touch with colleagues; it makes it so much easier to fit back in. When I was on maternity leave with my daughter, Isabella, I basically turned my living room into a drop-in for coffee and cake for my team on a Friday morning; it meant I could stay in touch, but in an informal way, and that I was abreast of all the issues when I went back, which massively helped with my confidence. Then, when you're ready to go back to work, just be aware that very often the first few months are challenging, and you need to rethink how you work most effectively.

Michelle Kennedy took five months off after the birth of her son, Finn, and said because she was the first senior person in the organisation to have a baby, that when she returned, 'I had this attitude that I wanted to prove to everyone that nothing had changed since I'd become a mother.' It stemmed from a lack of confidence. 'If someone wanted to have a conference call at 7pm, I'd say yes, even though that was bedtime, because I felt guilty going home. Or I would say yes to events after work that I didn't really want to go to. It took me a long time to have the confidence to say you can contact me for work at any time, save for the hours 5.30–7pm, when I'm putting Finn to bed, then I'm all yours again and I'll happily work till whatever time you need me. I realised that what I was doing was a huge disservice to me and also to any other woman behind me who felt they had to do the same.'

The key lesson is that it's OK to set boundaries – in fact, it's important to do so to avoid burnout and establish a work/life balance that works for you. We'll discuss boundaries further in chapter seven.

But also, when you go back to work, make sure there are other women who can support you in the transition. 'I have always been lucky to have a strong base of female friends in my business,' Nancy Josephson, partner at Endeavor agrees. 'We talk and meet frequently and give each other advice on everything from working motherhood to navigating office politics. These relationships are nurtured by supporting one another in good times and bad.' Marisa Thalberg, CMO of Taco Bell, went one step further and set up a formal support group for returning mothers, called Executive Moms, which she ran for 13 years. 'It was less about pedantic advice and much more about seeing other women to whom you relate and aspire. It is the feeling of not being alone in your experience and really, the self-affirmation that can come with that. That, and of course the good ideas and real connections that might ensue.'

8. Increase your knowledge

As well as knowing your existing strengths, increasing your knowledge massively helps with confidence. If you feel that you're inexperienced in any area, then think about how to upskill yourself. Work out what kind of professional development you need, be it help reaching a specific goal, to plug a skill gap or something technical or interpersonal. Once you've identified it you can then tap into company training resources, online courses such as the free AllBright Academy or General Assembly, which bills itself as a 'global education network for entrepreneurs' and offers practical training courses. Additionally, there are many specific courses available, like Think Digital, which offers social media lessons, B-School for marketing and Udacity for programming skills.

If you need to pay for a course personally, think of it as an investment rather than an expense (and remember if you're self-employed that investment may be tax deductible). If you need to make a business case to your boss, think about how to present it. You have to prove the expense will benefit the organisation, so spend some time researching it, collating reviews and feedback and factoring in the cost.

Continued professional development is especially important for those who work flexibly, as is becoming increasingly common. According to research by the UK flexible recruitment consultancy firm Timewise, 25 per cent of flexible workers who spend time out of the office feel that they have access to fewer opportunities such as extra training. For those returning to the workplace after a career gap – be that maternity leave, redundancy, ill health, raising children or caring for relatives – it's hugely helpful to upskill, particularly around new technologies. If everyone in your company uses Slack to message instead of email, Asana to assign team tasks, or Google Hangouts instead of physical meetings, you need to be confident about using them too. Technology is moving at an increasing pace and it's essential to business. Kathryn Parsons, whose business Decoded has so far helped over 100,000 employees of Fortune 500 companies learn to code, is passionate about women learning to code: 'The future is written in lines of code, and women need to be a part of that,' she says.

9. Take risks

Taking risks is a crucial part of achieving your career ambitions. If you take a big risk and it works out, your self-belief will soar. The interior designer Kelly Hoppen says she's always taken risks. 'I think I've always been quite direct! From day one, when given the opportunity to design without much experience, I just went for it and learned very quickly along the way. You have to have confidence and belief in your ability.'

But a fear of failure was the biggest concern of female founders according to a study from the private business school, Babson College, based in Wellesley, Massachusetts. It really shouldn't be. We've found that you've got to put yourself out there and try new ideas, and if some don't work out, then that's a lesson learned. Indeed, it's a popular business philosophy – as Jeff Bezos wrote in his letter to Amazon shareholders in 2016, noting that the company became the fastest ever to reach $100 billion in annual sales: 'I believe we are the best place in the world to fail (we have plenty of practice!), and failure and invention are inseparable twins. To invent you have to experiment, and if you know in advance that it's going to work, it's not an experiment … Given a ten per cent chance of a 100 times payoff, you should take that bet every time. But you're still going to be wrong nine times out of ten.'

Failures happen to all of us in life and in business – and you do need to build up resilience to deal with the big setbacks, which we'll discuss in detail in chapter eight. But the thought of failure shouldn't put you off trying. Because taking risks and seeing them work out is amazing for your confidence.

10. Find your cheerleaders

You need your sisterhood to act as your cheerleaders. This can have the single biggest impact on your confidence. When we surveyed our AllBright members, 65 per cent of them said they feel most confident when meeting like-minded people. 'When you feel that you are part of a cohort, you feel greater than the sum of your parts,' says Sarah Wood, who founded her tech company when Debbie was starting out with Love Home Swap, and is part of Debbie's sisterhood. 'It gives you confidence. You know that you can step up for each other when you need to.' Olivia Wollenberg, founder of Livia's Kitchen, who is still at the start of her career, has found this, too. 'It is sometimes hugely comforting to know that your brand peers are encountering similar problems and we can all offer the best advice to each other,' she says.

I feel hugely lucky to have found a business partner and friend in Debbie. We are each other's support, cheerleader and driver. 'It is the feeling of not being alone in your experience and really, the self-affirmation that can come with that,' says Marisa Thalberg.

Building a network is essential to confidence. Once you've got a solid team in your corner you feel you're supported from all angles, from bouncing crazy ideas off them, to learning about how they approach situations differently to you, to having a team that can cheer you on. As Michelle Jubelirer, COO of Capitol Music Group, says: 'My tribe of ladies root for each other both professionally and personally. We push each other to take risks even when they are scary.' It's such a useful tactic.

When Barack Obama entered the White House, his team of top aides was overwhelmingly male, so female staffers began using what they called an 'amplification' tactic to boost their collective female voices. They said that they started repeating each other's suggestions, to make sure they were being listened to, while crediting the speaker. 'We just started doing it and made a purpose of doing it. It was an everyday thing,' one aide told the *Washington Post*. The result? During Obama's second term, his top advisors were balanced almost equally between men and women.

It's a powerful tactic. Women can often find themselves pitted against each other, but our experience is that by sidling up to the most impressive girl at the party – as we did – it can help transform your career in new and unexpected ways.

CASE STUDY: SINÉAD BURKE, AUTHOR, ACADEMIC AND ACTIVIST

If you've watched TED speakers and wondered how they master their fears, then Sinéad Burke, whose TED talk, 'Why Design Should Include Everyone', which addressed the need for product design to consider those with disabilities, has been viewed by more than 1.3 million people, reinforces that nerves happen to everyone. 'I'd love to tell you that the rehearsal for my TED talk went well, but it was the antithesis of this,' she says. 'During the rehearsal I forgot two sections, I got the order wrong, I even said to the audience, I don't know where I am. The organisers were really worried about it.'

Her talk was part of her personal crusade to make the world's able-bodied designers and architects think about those who are not physically the same as them. At 105 centimetres (or three feet, five inches) tall, she's found that many simple things, from the height of a lock in a public toilet and the range of available shoe sizes, even to how networking events are organised, with everyone standing up leaving her unable to hear, inhibit her ability to participate. It was an important message that she needed to spread.

Sinéad needed to be able to find her inner confidence. 'An hour before the talk, I had to lock myself in the disabled bathroom and coach myself into going through with it. I told myself two things: "No one can do this better than you – this is your story, and based on that alone it has merit, it has value. It's right that you contribute." And, "You're making yourself nervous over the possibility that something good might come from this. What's the worst that can happen? It goes awfully, fine, you'll learn something from it. But by embracing this and revelling in the opportunity, something good might come from it."'

Watching her inspirational final talk, you wouldn't guess that she'd nearly not been able to deliver it, and her pep talk is an inspirational one we should all remember.

CHAPTER RECAP: The 10-step Confidence Plan

Everyone, even the most competent, pulled-together-looking woman, suffers crises of confidence. But there are tips and tricks to get you through them.

Preparation: You can't fake it if you don't know your stuff. Study ahead of time.

Own your space: Fight the urge to want to disappear into the background. Instead, act confidently and own your space. Adopt a modified version of a power pose and own your voice, don't start a sentence with an apology.

Deep breathing: Taking a deep breath is a simple form of meditation that will calm you down, as well as strengthening your brain's fight or flight centre. By practising your breathing work, you'll find you can also be more calm in the future.

Connect with your audience: Direct attention away from yourself and any nerves you might have by focusing on your core message, and what your audience really wants.

Banish imposter syndrome: We all feel it, but remember it's manageable. Take the sting out of its tail by sharing your feelings with someone in your network and treating your inner critic with compassion.

Career breaks: Coming back from any time off can dent your confidence. But remember that you've been working far longer than you've been off – you will remember how to do your job again.

Increase your knowledge: A lack of confidence comes from a fear of not being good enough, so upskill yourself. There is a plethora of courses that can help plug any gaps.

Take risks: Risks are essential to growth, personally and for a business, and when you pull them off, they are huge boosts to your confidence. You have to be prepared to fail and see it as a by-product of experimentation. And know that's OK.

Find your cheerleaders: Use your support network to test out your ideas, practise a presentation and to cheer you on when you need a boost.

WORKSHEET: GAINING CONFIDENCE

We all suffer from imposter syndrome at points in our careers – it's time to banish it. Research tells us that to override our brain's natural negativity, we need to have five times the number of positive messages to each self-critical thought. It's time now to celebrate your achievements. Write down five positive messages about your business self. What are you best at? Note a time that you've been brave and taken a risk. What do other people admire in you?

Celebrate it here:

1 _____

2 _____

3 _____

4 _____

5 _____

CHAPTER FOUR

The Entrepreneurial Mindset

'The woman who can create her own job is the woman who will win fame and fortune'

Amelia Earhart

Debbie

My route to becoming an entrepreneur started early. I saw my mother and grandmother run their own businesses, and it just felt natural that I would do the same. I honed my skills at a young age. When I was 15, in the Young Enterprise programme at my school, I had an award-winning hair scrunchie business (it was the eighties!). After a brief spell as a management consultant, I quickly realised I wanted to work for myself – as my mum and grandmother had done.

So, in 1999, when I was 25, I co-founded my first business, a communications agency called Mantra. I ran it for seven years and had the challenge not only of being a 25-year-old woman who was recruiting and leading people older than myself, learning the rules of business on the job, but shortly after I founded my digital company, the bottom fell out of the internet when the dotcom bubble burst. It was, to put it lightly, a turbulent time. More than half of digital businesses globally folded, and after the Nasdaq index of technology shares peaked in March 2000, it went on to lose 80 per cent of its value in two years – about $5 trillion. We weathered the storm – just. There were plenty of spine-tingling moments when we nearly ran out of money (as I almost have in every company I've ever founded) and it was a huge lesson in how to be an entrepreneur and how to run a business. I sold that company in 2007 and was itching to try something new.

The next flash of inspiration struck while I was on a plane home from a holiday, trying to half watch a film while entertaining my two young children, both under three. The film was *The Holiday*, in which Cameron Diaz and Kate Winslet's characters swap homes and lives. I'd just endured an impractical, frustrating stay in a hotel with my children, and on screen was exactly the trip that I wished I could have had, with the ease of being in someone else's home in a foreign country. I instantly saw a gap in the market – I knew there must be other people like me who would want that same home-from-home experience. I couldn't leave the idea alone, and so Love Home Swap was born. I recruited my younger brother Ben to work with me on the idea and, over the next five years, Love Home Swap took off during a time when the so-called 'sharing economy' was really gaining traction. We built the business, starting from abso-lutely nothing, as most start-ups do, to eventually selling it for $53 million in July 2017 to Wyndham Destination Network.

Just before I sold Love Home Swap, in 2015, I met Anna at a party. As our friendship developed, we kept returning to the issue that had been the soundtrack to both of our careers – why weren't there more women starting and leading businesses? A few months down the line we realised that out of this frustration we could see an opportunity for us to make a difference (entrepreneurs love frustrations – it means there's a chance for us to build something to solve the problem). And so we started working on our company, AllBright.

Anna's story is different. She worked her way up within big companies until she reached the very top – but she credits an entrepreneurial spirit with getting her there. Indeed, according to a survey by Accenture, 93 per cent of business executives believe innovation is fundamental to driving lasting success. There's a moniker for those who employ innovation and an entrepreneurial creativity within a larger company: 'intrapreneurs'. When she reached the top of the career ladder, as CEO with a corner office and a staff of thousands, running a portfolio of more than 25 businesses, she had an overwhelming urge to scratch that entrepreneurial itch and start a business of her own. Our career paths have been very different, but they show that entrepreneurial spirit can be developed at all times of life.

This chapter is all about harnessing that entrepreneurial spirit – something everyone, no matter what sphere of business or society they are in, should do. It's about embracing the skills that are typically associated with entrepreneurs, such as a strong sense of vision, dogged hard graft and creative flair. Whatever your budget and whatever your business or position, these are all essential skills and critical success factors.

What you'll learn in this chapter:

- How to spot opportunities – and chase them down
- To stick true to your vision
- How restrictions can encourage creativity
- To take a calculated risk
- How your network can help you to think like an entrepreneur

What is the entrepreneurial mindset?

The entrepreneurial mindset is an attitude, a state of being, a way of solving problems. We define it as meaning that you're always challenging the status quo. While perhaps it comes more naturally to some than others, it's something we can all learn. If we're going to challenge the alarming stat that there are more men called John leading top firms than there are women (currently true of the UK, USA and Australia), we need to be a bit more creative about our approach. And an entrepreneurial mindset is crucial to success.

Lots of brilliant ideas are born out of frustration. Just as Love Home Swap had its roots in feeling like there was a better way to take a family holiday, many other successful entrepreneurs mine the feeling that there are problems to be solved. Because if you think something is lacking or wrong or broken, chances are others do too.

Think of Sara Blakely, who founded Spanx when she was 29 because she wanted flattering underwear to wear underneath a pair of white trousers. Forbes now estimates her net worth at more than $1 billion. Those fortune-inspiring trousers are in a glass display case at Spanx HQ in Atlanta; a visual reminder of a frustration that proved very fruitful.

Or what about New York businesswomen Steph Korey and Jen Rubio – both former executives at Warby Parker and Forbes 30 Under 30 alumni? Their suitcase brand Away, which has been spotted on well-travelled celebrities from Karlie Kloss and Jessica Alba to Margot Robbie, was inspired by frustration over a lack of stylish luggage. The lightbulb moment came when Jen's suitcase fell apart while she was travelling and she needed a quick – and not wallet-busting – replacement.

It's not just in the business world where a sense of frustration drives an entrepreneurial mindset. When Clara Hemphill, a Pulitzer Prize-winning journalist, began looking for a New York City public school for her son, she realised there was a lack of information for parents. So, she founded the website InsideSchools.org, which gives the inside scoop on each of the city's 1,500 public schools, including admissions processes, teaching styles, homework and discipline to help parents make an informed and empowered decision. The *New Yorker* named her in the top 200 most influential New Yorkers for her initiative.

In the UK, a primary school headteacher in Scotland has been credited with transforming the lives of millions of children around the world, and potentially coming up with a solution to the obesity crisis. All because of a frustration. When Elaine Wyllie realised one day that her young pupils were unfit, she decided to make the class she was covering walk around the school field – outside the traditional PE lesson – for 15 minutes. She gradually extended this to the whole school, asking children to start running when they felt fit enough. Within just four weeks, Edinburgh University scientists have documented, fitness levels had dramatically increased, attention levels and behaviour in class were improved and parents commented that their children were more active and alert, and were sleeping much better. 'None of it was planned,' Elaine says. 'I just took them outside one day for a run around.' Proof, if it were needed, that the best ideas are often the simplest; and they can happen in any organisation.

Spotting opportunities

It's not just frustrations that can spark ideas – entrepreneurs are always on the lookout for opportunities. 'To be a successful entrepreneur you have to go out there and grab every opportunity that is given to you,' Kathryn Parsons, CEO of Decoded points out. Consider the famous instance of Jack Ma, who taught English in his native China, and who had little business experience. In 1998, while on a trip to Seattle, he first saw a computer connected to the internet. He typed in 'beer' and saw results pop up from all over the world, except China. He realised that none of China's small and medium-sized businesses were represented on the internet, so he created what would become the $216-billion Alibaba. It just shows you don't need to already be an entrepreneur to harness the mindset and spot opportunities.

Joanna Coles, executive producer, says all of this applies just as much if you're working in a big company. 'The exciting thing about a career is that opportunity leads to opportunity. It's about staying open to unexpected ideas and invitations and people that lead in all sorts of directions you could never have imagined. I am all for loose plans with the expectation that you must stay flexible and the best laid plans can change at any moment.'

Anna says that an entrepreneurial spirit was key to her personal success – and those around her. She had been brought in to rethink radically what a media company could do, and she needed a visionary team to support her. It meant thinking beyond what had traditionally been expected of magazines in an era when print sales were slowing. So, the title *Men's Health* started producing its own-brand gym equipment, and *Country Living* launched a range of sofas and chairs. The people who spotted the opportunities within her team were the ones who secured promotions. If you can always think how that entrepreneurial spirit can help your business, you will absolutely fly.

Making it happen

You've got the idea. Well done. But as Joy Mangano, the US inventor with over $3 billion in sales of products like the Miracle Mop (and who was played by Jennifer Lawrence in the film about her life), says: 'So many people say "I have a great idea"; it's the execution behind that. You must know that you don't have to be an expert in something to get started. Sometimes the simplest things change lives; it doesn't have to be rocket ships. I was a mom with three little children and I designed a mop.' You've just got to do it.

Lorraine Candy, who worked for Anna at Hearst when she was editor of *ELLE* UK, and who is now luxury content director at the *Sunday Times* and editor-in-chief of *Style* magazine, is known in the industry for her entrepreneurial spirit and tireless work ethic. She agrees that ideas are one thing, but it's all about getting it done. 'When I moved my editorial team at *ELLE* from working on just print content to working across all our platforms and into a hot desk environment (unheard of for a glossy at that time), I had to employ a very entrepreneurial spirit,' she says. 'This innovation was so new we had to move around all the rocks in the stream of our traditional workflow, or the project would have taken a year to complete.' It was a huge success that not only benefited the company, but also future-proofed every member of the team's CVs. But it couldn't have happened without Lorraine's entrepreneurial drive.

Sticking to a vision

Cath Kidston, founder of her eponymous homewares brand, sold for an estimated £75 million in 2010, was already a successful interior designer when she left her comfortable job to start her business in 1993. 'I had a lot of people saying, "why are you taking a risk?"' It was not an overnight success, 'But I did have an absolute passion and belief – a naïve belief I think now – in my own idea.' She says she had a very strong and clear concept of what she wanted to sell, which was something no one else at the time was doing. 'I had a vision of cheerful, affordable, practical homeware products. I had a really clear brand ethos. I sacrificed margin to get the product to be the right price. I sacrificed a lot of things to put brand first and sales were slow to start. But the one thing I remember thinking, was that if I protect the brand and keep it focused it will be recognised. I really focused on building something for the future.'

It's a lesson all of us in business can draw on, whatever our product, service or idea – the vision and purpose that we worked on in chapter two is central to your success. As you grow and get different stakeholders interested in the direction of your business, it becomes even more vital to stick to what you believe in. That doesn't mean dismissing advice, or not flexing, but carefully evaluating what's being suggested. Don't do that on your own – you need to get advice from your sisterhood; people who care about you and your success but can see the business objectively, too.

Dogged hard work

While the traditional narrative of entrepreneurs is that they are all geniuses, actually that's not always true. Sure, you need business smarts, but common sense and hard work are much more important than genius genes. Behind every over-night success there are so many hours of graft.

Sometimes that means working around the clock, because the truth is, as an entrepreneur and business founder, there's no one who cares about your product as much as you do. Anna says that this was true for her in the corporate world, too and that at Hearst she cared about the company as much as a founder did. She believes that it was her tendency to 'put my hand up for everything' and her hard work that led to her rise up the ranks to CEO. Similarly other people who surrounded her and acted with the same level of hard work and dedication were the ones who got promoted.

We're not advocating working until burnout. You have to find your own balance – and we'll be delving into this more in chapter seven. But you need to know that you've done all you can that day to drive your idea and your business forward.

Refusal to give up

Part of this can be not giving up, even when the idea – or the business – seems doomed. 'There are days when you think maybe my idea is really bad,' Trinny Woodall, the television presenter who has recently become an entrepreneur and launched her own beauty line, Trinny London, confesses, 'but I will go to bed thinking I will fight another day. I never think I'm going to give up.' That way of thinking has been absolutely crucial to our success; there are plenty of days when things are tough and you just have to pull your shoulders back and face the day ahead.

Cath Kidston remembers an early 'disaster' that could have floored her. 'When I first started, I had a small budget and I ordered a lot of bed linen from Eastern Europe. But when it arrived it was all the wrong sizes, so I had palettes of duvet covers outside my shop that were all unsaleable. I ended up sitting on a mound of fabric, thinking, "what am I going to do?"'

She didn't give up, but also she employed another entrepreneurial mindset trick and thought her way out of the problem. 'I cut up the fabric and made small products and really I built the business accidentally. It was one of those classic times when actually a disaster can work in your favour.'

We've found that too. There is usually always a way around a 'no', another way to approach it, another time to try your idea – you just have to get creative. Your business will almost certainly not be what you thought it was when you started. Every company I've ever founded, including AllBright, has turned out to be something different, and you have to be open to change.

Working on a shoestring budget

It's well known that entrepreneurs often work on a shoe-string budget, with limited staff, resources and support – we certainly have at various points in our career. But it happens in big business, too. Farrah Storr was the deputy editor of a women's magazine when she was approached to be the launch editor of a new title in the UK: *Women's Health* magazine. It had a strong brand presence in the US and a successful, established brother title, *Men's Health*, so there was a lot at stake. 'I had a staff of two, very limited budget and six weeks to make an issue and we had to sell 100,000 copies in the first issue,' she says. The magazine achieved that and more: '*Women's Health* went on to be the magazine launch of the decade.'

Two years later, she was asked to do the impossible again: turn around the well-established, but failing maga-zine *Cosmopolitan* UK by relaunching it and returning it to its spot as the bestselling women's magazine. This time she had eight weeks, but again a staff shortage, as 80 per cent of her staff had resigned. Once again, she did it – *Cosmo* went back to its number one spot. 'What I learned was that the two major significant high points in my career were when I was given very difficult jobs to do, and the magic in your career happens at moments where you feel challenged and pushed,' she says. 'Constraints of time, money and resources unlock creativity.' We've found that too; we're always brimming with ideas about how to spread our message, so we've launched the online academy, a magazine, this book and new clubs – all in a short space of time. Lots of people said it couldn't be done.

How to harness this in your own career? If your boss has given you four weeks to deliver on something, try to finish it in two weeks – the less time you have, the more you trust your gut instinct and you come up with big outlandish and creative ideas. That is at the heart of the entrepreneurial mindset.

Use your sisterhood

There's a myth that circulates about the successful entrepreneur: that they are a lone wolf. But actually, many of the entrepreneurs we know about had teammates. Steve Jobs had his co-founder Steve Wozniak and the designer Jony Ive as his wingmen; Bill Gates was supported by his co-founder Paul Allen. Personally, I've had huge success working in partnerships with the co-founders of my early businesses, with my brother and now Anna. The point is, there are lots of partnerships and collaborations involved in entrepreneurship, so don't feel like you need to do it alone to achieve success.

While Lorraine Candy was the editor-in-chief of *ELLE*, she needed the support of her whole team to pull off the shift in strategy that she described earlier. It's a great example of how your work sisterhood can help – even when you're the boss. 'I chose to work with people who had the right enthusiasm and appetite for change and asked them to be cheerleaders for me,' she says. 'I knew the energy needed to get everyone on board had to come from both the top of the tree and the bottom, so I chose assistants and team members whose roles may not have been obviously suited to carrying out the actual work to help me, but I knew they would enthuse an entire team really quickly to get everyone on board.' The diversity within her team meant that the project was a success.

When you start out, you need favours from everyone. You'll be surprised how many people in your existing network will be able and willing to help you out on your entrepreneurial journey – and we'll talk more about this in chapter twelve. It pays to do the same back and return favours and help contacts out – you might need to draw on them again in the future. We founded AllBright with the help of a very special girl gang who believe in our vision for an eco-system for working women, and we've been overwhelmed with the support they've given us. Lots of our friends have been investors or founding members of our clubs, while wider members of our sisterhood have generously given their time and expertise to deliver lectures on the AllBright Academy. Believe us when we say that we know and truly rate the value of female support, friendship and inspiration, and recognise how important it has been to our entrepreneurial careers – and can be to yours, too.

There are lots of lessons to learn about the entrepreneurial mindset, both inside a corporation and as a founder. Here are two very different women on different career paths who want to share how to harness an entrepreneurial mindset:

CASE STUDY: SAHAR HASHEMI OBE, CO-FOUNDER COFFEE REPUBLIC

Sahar doesn't describe herself as a natural business founder. She says she hadn't displayed any entrepreneurial spirit at school, as many founders had, and she had gone from a law degree straight into a firm. However, she didn't feel suited to the job, so when her father died, prompting a big life change, she quit her job and travelled to America on a holiday. It was there she had a flash of entrepreneurial inspiration. She noticed that there were lots of speciality coffee shops all over the country, yet when she returned to the UK, she saw there were none. On one day of research, she spent five hours getting off at tube stops all over London just to check her theory and found no bespoke coffee bars. Seeing a gap in the market – and a frustration at not being able to get a skinny cappuccino on demand – she 'took a leap and started a business with my brother'. Although they had no experience of being in business, together they launched the UK's first US-style coffee bar chain, Coffee Republic in 1995. 'We thought the fact that we knew nothing was a problem, but actually, looking back, it was an advantage,' she says.

Not least because they didn't know how tough it was going to be. They immersed themselves in research; she says they nearly killed themselves by tasting 26 coffees in a day. It was also a slog to raise finance. They had to make 40 loan applications to borrow £90,000 to open their first coffee bar, and only got one 'yes'; they were continually told that the UK is a nation of tea drinkers (note to those investors: the UK now drinks 95 million cups of coffee a year, according to the Centre for Economics and Business Research).

Then, when they started, sales were slow. Sahar recalls how her mother was gallantly buying as many drinks as she could, but that the public were not used to the idea of coffee drinking. But the siblings' vision and dedication paid off. After six years, in 2001, having built up an empire of 108 shops, they both sold their shares in the company. Sahar has gone on to write three books about entrepreneurship, as well as giving TED talks and lectures around the world.

Her big passion is showing people how that the entre-preneurial spirit that she harnessed in the early days of her start-up is essential to success in any business, whatever its size. She says that these days, 'The crosswinds of disruption at the moment are so huge that all of us had to think like a start-up.'

One of the main lessons, she says, is the importance of being clueless. 'When you're out of your comfort zone, you become curious and ask the naïve questions. When you've got that curious mind, it's about boot-strapping [start-ing a business without external help or finance], it's about extreme experimentation – trying small things out the whole time, trial and error. Perfectionism is the enemy of that.'

CASE STUDY ANTONIA ROMEO, SENIOR CIVIL SERVANT IN HER MAJESTY'S CIVIL SERVICE

Antonia Romeo is the Permanent Secretary of the Department for International Trade for the UK Government, a department which helps businesses export and grow into global markets. Before this, she was Her Majesty's Consul General in New York, but she started her career in the private sector, at strategic consultancy firm Oliver Wyman. She is passionate about helping women advance their careers and, like Anna, believes that an entrepreneurial mindset is crucial to climbing the career ladder. 'Mindset really matters,' she says. 'It's all about having a positive attitude to what you're doing and the opportunities ahead. You have to spot opportunities and then be confident to put your hand up, otherwise they will pass you by. You're the person in control of your own career.' That can be things that are directly related to your job, or to improve the organisation, such as getting involved in the diversity network. Antonia explains, 'It's a good way to demonstrate to senior people that you're enthusiastic and want to make a contribution.'

Networking, she says, is crucial to this: 'You've got to be operating different networks at the same time. You have to assume that everyone you meet has something great to offer. If you are positive and open in the way you are with them, you never know who's going to be a crucial person to help you later achieve something. And you'll be that person for them.'

Your network can be vital in helping you be more entrepreneurial with your career, she says. She remembers a time when she was working compressed hours after the birth of her first child and wanted to go for a promotion to the senior civil service. 'There was a person mentoring me who told me I was good enough to go for it. Having someone telling me, you are good enough, they should take you and backing you was so important to me.'

CHAPTER RECAP: The Entrepreneurial Mindset

The entrepreneurial mindset is something that's useful for all of us to tap into, whether we're freelancers, founding our own companies, working our way up from inside or leading and shaping FTSE 100s.

Spotting opportunities: Frustration is a great source of inspiration to entrepreneurs. Think of something that you feel is lacking in your daily life or working practice, and there's a chance that others could need that product or service, too. Any glimmers of opportunities can inspire you. That could be volunteering for jobs at work that lead to career boosts or seeing gaps in the market.

Hard work: Entrepreneurs put so much hard work into their product because there's often no other way to get the idea off the ground – it's all down to them. If you adopt a similar attitude in your role, it will pay off.

Refusal to give up: There's often another way around the problem. Attack it from a different angle, try again at a different time. Don't accept your first no.

Working within restrictions: Entrepreneurs have tight time frames, budgets and staff numbers, and from those restrictions, creativity can soar. Try imposing restrictions on your next project – time or costs – and you'll be amazed at the results.

Tapping into your network: When you're starting out you need favours from everyone to help you grow, and you soon realise the talent within your network. Don't be afraid to ask for help – and offer favours in return.

WORKSHEET: How to develop an entrepreneurial mindset

We've heard from some amazing entrepreneurial women, all with very different experiences and tips, from Lorraine Candy motivating her whole team to help cheerlead her entrepreneurial project through to completion, to Antonia Romeo's belief that a positive attitude and a refusal to give up are key, to Sahar Hashemi who thinks that curiosity and naïvety are essential to success. Take a look back over the chapter summary and pick four key entrepreneurial attitudes you are going to adopt. List them here, with an example of what steps you can take next.

Entrepreneurial attitude no.1

_____

Put that into action:

_____

_____

_____

_____

Entrepreneurial attitude no.2

_____

Put that into action:

_____

_____

_____

_____

Entrepreneurial attitude no.3

_____

Put that into action:

_____

_____

_____

_____

Entrepreneurial attitude no.4

_____

Put that into action:

_____

_____

_____

_____

BUILD.

By now you should be feeling confident in who you are, what matters to you and what you want to achieve. This section is about putting what you've learned in *Believe* into action. You need to establish and communicate a strong personal brand, something that is recognisably you. It's just as essential to entrepreneurs as those working in corporations and the same principles apply: your brand is something that people can believe and invest in, be it their money, their time or their business. It's essential to understand your brand when expanding your network. The next part of your business toolkit is getting to grips with all the details and operations of your company, whether you're a founder or an employee. You don't have to do it alone: reach out to your work sisterhood for help. Finally, work can be all-consuming; at times it needs to be. But it's essential to build up your wellness strategy together with your resilience to keep you at the top of your game. If we don't take care of ourselves, we'll end up burnt out. Work on your support strategy – and sisterhood – for protection.

CHAPTER FIVE

Constructing Your Personal Brand

'Life isn't about finding yourself. Life is about creating yourself'

George Bernard Shaw

Anna

Building up a personal brand is something successful people do almost effortlessly. Some have a trademark way of dressing – think Anna Wintour's bobbed hair and kitten heels combo, or Mark Zuckerberg's famous grey hoodie uniform. For others, it's a message they feel really connected to and are skilled at communicating, like Arianna Huffington on the power of sleep. 'Personal branding is about managing your name – even if you don't own a business,' as American author and entrepreneur Tim Ferriss has said.

Your personal brand is your business armour – it's how you get recognised and remembered. It is shorthand for everything you stand for. It's a succinct summary encapsulating your core values, strengths and your USPs – all things we worked on in *Believe*. But more than that, it's your personality, your leadership style and your communication style – both in what you say verbally and how you communicate visually through body language and clothes. Some of these qualities are innate to you – your personality for example – but other areas you can mould and shape to help you get to the top, like working on your communication style.

I've found building my own personal brand essential to my success. The key to working out what your own tag line is, is a strong sense of self-awareness. Over the years I've worked out that I'm known for being honest and direct, but warm and empathetic, too. I'm hard-working and good at spotting opportunities for growth. In a nutshell, my personal brand is that I'm warm, direct and a fast decision maker, but with inner steel. What's yours? That's what we'll work on in this chapter.

Of course, branding isn't just about what you believe and how you work – it's about how you project yourself to the outside world. Exactly *how* you communicate your core message is very much part of your personal brand. Are you assertive, passive or aggressive? You have to make a choice and work on the style that you want to embody because your communication style says a lot about you. I choose to be assertive, and suggest you should be too. It means tapping into your empathy, working out the best way to get your message across to your listener, being honest, direct and con-fident, while listening and responding to their speech and cues. It's an art form.

I'm authentic in the way I talk to people, but not to the point where I overshare, and this has been central to helping me lead a team. I told you in chapter three about the senior woman in my team who came into my meetings late and was nervous to voice her opinions, despite being one of the most talented people there. Once we worked on her communication style together, her confidence quickly rose and she ended up being promoted a few months later. Once you've mastered this, you need to learn how to flex your style, depending on what stakeholders you're addressing. The whole point of communicating is that your message is heard – so you have to work out how to make that happen.

As I mentioned, the first thing you picture about people like Anna Wintour or Mark Zuckerberg is often their clothes. It's not just a female issue, our clothes and how we present ourselves matters for everyone. There are countless studies that show the first impression people make about you is a visual one. One study showed it even had an effect on your performance: incredibly, athletes wearing the colour red were able to lift a heavier weight than when they were wearing blue.

There's no doubt that clothes affect our psychology. When I was suddenly thrust into the role of CEO, I needed to make sure I looked like I was in charge. I was younger than most of the people I managed, and I needed to project an aura of responsibility, polish and leadership. I have a slight frame so I thought about how I could project myself and how I could ensure I was on a visual par with the – often – men in the room. For me, this was wearing a blazer and heels. I have always thought about clothes as professional armour. I love fashion and working in magazines meant I never did the 'corporate suit' look, but I was aware that how I dressed was an important part of my personal brand. Look at other female leaders and CEOs and you'll see a similar picture. Christine Lagarde, for example, is known for her love of smart Chanel

Couture, and has topped *Vanity Fair*'s international best-dressed list.

The physical world is not the only place where you need to make a good impression. More and more of our time is spent online, so how you present yourself digitally is of huge importance. With the number of platforms out there, it can be a full-time job. I love digital media, and the key to successful brands is that they maintain the professional and editorial standards of their real-world counterparts. Make sure your online branding reflects you – and if you don't like it, change it, fast.

We all know how important branding is in the corporate world – it can make or break a business. The same goes for your career; its success partly depends on how you project yourself. It's time to start building that personal brand.

What you'll learn in this chapter:

- How self-awareness is crucial to building your brand
- To define your USP and elevator pitch
- How to project your personal brand
- To maintain authenticity and consistency
- To curate your online presence
- How to build your buzz

Building your self-awareness

Building a brand requires a high level of self-awareness because you need to know yourself inside out in order to hone your key personal message. It translates directly into business success because, in my experience, those who have an understanding of their own emotions, personality, strengths and weaknesses can better engage with employees and clients, and ultimately lead better.

It sounds easy but building up self-awareness is actually quite tough to do. You might think that you're already quite self-aware. According to a three-year study by organisational psychologist Dr Tasha Eurich, 95 per cent of us think we have good self-awareness, whereas actually only 10–15 per cent of us really have it. It stands to reason that you might need some help. As you've already worked through the exercises to build up your knowledge of your strengths and weaknesses, values and motivations, you're already on the way to self-awareness.

Like lots of CEOs and business leaders, I've done versions of the Myers-Briggs Type Indicator, which aims to translate the psychological types detailed by Jung into useful markers to measure yourself against.

But of equal value is finding that work sister, someone that Dr Eurich would call a 'loving critic'. She notes that women are often better than men at helping each other be that loving critic. Debbie and I are really good at it with each other. She is good at pointing out how, when we're in a room with investors, I'm a natural listener and very good at working out what each individual personality needs to make them feel valued, while she is a natural salesperson and leads with the negotiations. Equally, she has helped me realise that I have to get better at self-promotion as I've transitioned from the corporate world, where I was recognised as the CEO of a well-known business, rather than a 'brand' in my own right.

One useful starting point is to consider whether you lean towards introversion or extroversion. Neither is right or wrong – Susan Cain, author of *Quiet*, says that around one third to half of the world's population is an introvert. But, she says in her book, 'The trick for introverts is to honour their styles instead of allowing themselves to be swept up by prevailing norms.'

I'm one of those who tends towards the introvert side of the scale. I don't get my energy from performing to large crowds, as Debbie does, but it hasn't held me back in the slightest. I just have to be aware of that natural tendency and pour energy into developing that area when I need to. I spend most of my waking life with other people and to balance this I try and build in time (even if it's just 15 minutes a day) where I'm not with anyone or, even if I am, that I can be quiet (sometimes I quite literally run out of words!). It is helpful to know your natural personality preferences as each type has different strengths and weaknesses that you can harness and adapt, according to the situation.

Your USPs

What makes you the best person for the job? It's a question we want you to think about seriously. To help you get there we're going to ask you to list your key qualities in the worksheet at the end of the chapter, because it's an essential foundation for figuring out your personal brand. Can't think what yours are? You're not alone, according to Melanie Eusebe, entrepreneur and founder of the Black British Business Awards. 'I think women need to pay more attention to recognising their inherent value,' she says. It comes down to confidence, which, as we addressed in chapter three, is a career-long exercise. 'You need to consider what you have already brought to the company, as well as what you intend to bring,' she adds. It helps to be really specific. Sure, I'm hard-working, but lots of people are. If I were to specify exactly, I know that one of my USPs is that I'm able to think about complex business decisions and distil them down, simply. If identifying these USPs feels like a struggle, try looking from the outside in and thinking about what words other people would use to describe you. This is the foundation of your brand and it is key to getting ahead.

What's a unique way of standing out? Often, it's our gender. There have been lots of instances where I've been the only woman in the room, as is common at the top of business. As Helena Morrissey, head of personal investing at Legal & General, has said, 'I remember being in the running for a Fund Manager of the Year award. My competition wasn't just all male, but they were all men called Paul. The Pauls and I were invited to go to all the investment conferences and sit on all the panels. To this day, I'll never know if I won because I was the only one who could be easily identified! But it did teach me that there are advantages to standing out.'

Perhaps it's gender and race. When Beatriz Acevedo, president of the Acevedo Foundation, reflects on how she managed to raise $50 million for her start-up, with no connections in the venture capital world, she says, 'The thing I realise looking back is that I felt incredibly empowered to be different. I would walk into those board rooms and they were full of very nice white men. I knew [my] demographic better than they did and that obviously gave me a lot of confidence.' We absolutely felt the same when pitching to investors an idea for a business about promoting women in business. We'd been there, risen through the ranks and could see where the challenges for other women were – and where we could help. That was our USP.

Beatriz says this mindset applies to anyone 'raising money or even applying for a job; as a woman or a person of colour, you need to know there's so much value and worth in being different, because you bring a new perspective.' It's an incredibly empowering mentality to adopt.

Crafting your elevator pitch

We talked in chapter four about the lessons you can learn from an entrepreneurial mindset, and this is an additional tip to steal: have your elevator pitch ready and waiting. It's a short, prepared statement about who you are and what you're good at, drawing on your USPs. Think of it like a dating profile; it does the same job. You're trying to sum up your best bits and explain why they – the investor, the boss, the hiring committee – should pick you.

Two women who became instant legends for their elevator pitch are Elizabeth Uviebinené and Yomi Adegoke, who wrote *Slay in Your Lane: The Black Girl Bible*. They had no publishing experience or contacts, but ended up in a nine-publisher bidding war with everyone desperate to buy their book. They've since been described as the 'Queens of Pitches' and people are still talking about how incredible their opening shot was. So how did they do it? 'It's so essential to be able to describe yourself and your product in a few sentences,' Elizabeth explains. She says that they knew there was a gap in the market for their business book about the experiences of black women because they had felt it. But they needed to convince the largely white publishing world, too. 'You have to know the industry you're selling your story to, understand and communicate why it's valuable to them, and learn the lingo, even if you're an outsider, like we were. You have to research like crazy and be curious.'

Then learn to adapt your pitch. Elizabeth and Yomi's elevator pitch to the publishers was different to the pitch they made to the people they asked to interview for the book. 'It's crucial to know exactly what the other person's brand is, when you're writing that email or meet them at an event, so that you're ready to pitch yourself straight away. We'd say things like, "we know you're really passionate about XYZ, and that you've spoken about it on this platform, and that fits really well with our message".' Your elevator pitch is essential to highlighting where you've got common ground, creating connections and expanding your network.

Finding your communication style

The next step on your personal branding journey is how you communicate your core message. While we all have our own unique ways of expressing ourselves, there are a few key communication styles. 'You've got to know the strengths and weaknesses of your own style,' advises Karen Blackett OBE, who as country manager at the global advertising agency WPP, is one of the most important women in advertising in the UK, and who, we know, has a killer communication style.

Assertive communicators

As we already know, you don't need to be aggressive in your communication style. We've all been in meetings with those characters who speak over everyone else and shout down anyone who disagrees with them. It's seriously ineffective; people start to tune out.

There's a middle ground. It's where you become honest, open and direct when you're speaking. There is an art to being an effective communicator, one that comes with practice, but also from observing people in your work sister-hood who have the technique nailed. You need to draw on the lessons of self-awareness and employ your empathy so that you can gauge how the other person is likely to or does respond. You can be forthright without being a bully, but equally you need to be empathetic without being submissive. You can start small with little tips like not starting your sentence with an apology – be proud of what you've got to say. As I said, it is an art, but one that can be forever honed.

Arianna Huffington has a similar style to the one I see as part of my personal brand; she terms it 'compassionate directness' and it's a core foundation of her company Thrive Global. As Joey Hubbard, head of training at Thrive Global has said, 'We found if they know you care, you can say just about anything.' One trick is to turn phrases into state-ments that start with 'I'. So, for aggressive communicators, instead of saying 'You're wrong', say 'I disagree'. It instantly pulls the focus back into being an opinion, rather than a judgement.

Sarah Wood, co-founder of Unruly, says that empathy is key. 'You need to always think about the person on the other end of the conversation,' she says. The problem we face as a society is that empathy is on the decrease. A study by the University of Michigan found that since 2000, empathy in college students has dropped by 40 per cent. It's termed 'compassion fatigue'. Feeling empathetic is a skill that we all desperately need to cling on to, and if you struggle with it, remember this tip from Sarah: start each meeting with a personal question about the person opposite you. It's a powerful way of reminding them you care.

Non-verbal communication

There are non-verbal tricks you can employ, too, such as physically positioning yourself on the same level if one of you is standing or sitting (being eye to eye is as effective in business as it is with small children!). Volume of voice is also a really interesting power dynamic; sometimes the most softly spoken people are the most terrifyingly effective communicators. Don't gabble. As Professor Amy Cuddy says in *Presence: Bringing Your Boldest Self to Your Biggest Challenges*, 'We don't rush our words. We're not afraid to pause. We feel deserving of the time we're using. We even make more direct eye contact while we're speaking.'

Amy is also passionate about how we hold our bodies. You need to inhabit your own space and stand tall and proud. It's something we touched on in chapter three, but as Amy explains, 'When our body language is confident and open, other people respond in kind, unconsciously reinforcing not only their perception of us but also our perception of ourselves.'

Next up is giving a robust handshake – particularly if you're the only woman in a meeting full of men, as I've often been. Though it can be an odd habit to learn to pick up, because it is associated with how men greet each other, it's worth adopting. Neuroscience research shows that a strong handshake at the beginning of a meeting leads to a more favourable impression. It's a way to assert your confidence and a really easy win at the start of the meeting.

Equinox CEO Niki Leondakis has a powerful non-verbal trick that she's picked up after having had one too many frustrating meetings where she's the only woman in the room, and assumed to be subordinate to the man next to her. She says that when she goes into a meeting, she lays out her business cards on the table at the start, so that people know exactly who she is.

Practice makes perfect

Once you've got your communication style nailed, the author, academic and activist Sinéad Burke advises, 'Speak as much as you can – you'll regret it if you don't. If you have to pretend to be more confident than you are, then just do it.' She suggests that if you attend a big meeting and didn't manage to speak up, then you could email the meeting leader afterwards with feedback, so that your voice is on record. Next time speak up.

Another tip that I personally tried early in my career was role play. In one of the companies I worked at I saw an obvious gap for a senior leadership role and I wasn't on the board, but I thought that I should be. I decided to attend the next few board meetings as if I were in this role already. I thought about where I should sit – at the head of the table opposite the boss. I was very organised, knew which points I wanted to get across, made sure I looked the part and challenged people – in a friendly, but assertive way. It worked and very soon after I was promoted. It taught me such a powerful lesson early on: act the part and you'll become it.

The power of listening

Let's not forget that the true power of communication is actually in listening. 'In terms of communication, we think of our ability to speak and when to speak,' Sinéad says, 'but actually it's listening to what they say and also what they don't say.'

Aggressive communicators are often terrible listeners and it's such a weakness. Make sure you know how to 'actively listen', which is a technique used in counselling and conflict disputes, and is now being adopted by the business world. It involves paying attention to non-verbal cues such as maintaining eye contact and nodding to encourage the speaker, as well as asking leading questions. Or try summarising and repeating back what someone has just told you. It has the three-fold effect of showing you were really listening, checking you got it right and also buying you time to formulate an answer. Another key component of active listening is not jumping in to offer your opinion, instead waiting until the speaker is finished. Active listening is actually something that women are usually good at naturally, and it's a really key component of your business toolkit, but as we discussed in the first chapter, many of our strengths can benefit from being flexed and used more frequently.

Often, when a conversation begins, we feel we have to start talking immediately. Silence is one of the most powerful tools you can use – especially if you're in a difficult conversation or important negotiation. It can feel very uncomfortable at first but give it a go and you might find out a lot more about what someone's really thinking.

Flex that style

The reason for heightening your powers of listening and empathy is so that you can work out your audience and adapt your message and style. One of the most effective leaders I worked with was a man who could take his key message and present it in totally different ways, whether to the board of directors or at a staff meeting. It was so interesting to watch how he would say essentially the same thing, but with totally different delivery to ensure he captured the individuals' interest.

WPP's Karen Blackett, also a master at this, agrees: 'I've done well in my career because I'm able to flex my natural communication style and fit into that four minutes or so that you have to speak before people start tuning out.' She adds: 'I'm good at tuning in and talking to a CEO of a bank or record company or changing that to address someone who works with me. That's become part of my personal brand.'

There are scientific studies to back this up, showing that those who are emotionally intelligent or who can adapt their communication and behaviour style, often do better in their careers.

Elizabeth Uviebiné admits she has recently had to learn how to do this in her day job: 'As a marketing manager I was responsible for seeing a campaign through from start to finish, and relying on lots of people in the chain, from legal experts to the creative team. My boss once said to me, "You're really good at certain aspects of this, but what holds you back is when someone is not giving you what you want, you can't flex your style."' She says it was a real lightbulb moment: 'I realised that you really have to take people on the journey with you, and to do that you need to be able to concisely communicate who you are and what the work is. It's about storytelling.'

She says that once she understood she needed to adapt her communication style, she instantly became a better leader, and that played into her personal brand. 'Instead of just saying something doesn't work, I'd use language that empowered them to be able to change. I realised I could say the same thing, but in a different, more effective way. I learned to spell it out: this is where we are now, this is where we want to end up, these are the steps to get there.'

She's spot on when she says that you often have to spell it out. It can be frustrating, but I've found that you can't tell people the same message enough, because they don't always listen first time. What makes communication such a strong part of my personal brand is, I think, partly down to the fact that I've learned to repeat my message in different ways – be that catch-ups, walking meetings or company-wide presentations – until I'm sure it's sunk in.

Written communications

Don't forget that everything you write down should follow the same rules. What's the first glimpse an employer has of you and your personal brand? Your CV. You need to think carefully about the design and content, but what we want to flag is your choice of language. According to research on the gender pay gap, women's disadvantages start here because we engage in passive communication from the get-go. A study found that twice as many women described their work using terms such as 'involved', 'participated', 'exposed to' or – even more vaguely – 'working on'. Men, on the other hand, often used more dynamic words like 'creating', 'producing' or 'leading'. Remember this, not just when you're writing your CV, but every time you email someone or prepare a company presentation. Because it literally pays to be assertive in your choice of written communications, too.

Maintaining authenticity

Authenticity is becoming really important in business. Whole books have been written on the topic, but at its core, being authentic means being yourself and upholding the values you believe in. If you think of the most success-ful business leaders, companies and brands, then one of the key attributes they share is authenticity. It displays an inner confidence that you know who the person or what the brand is, and what they stand for. At its core, authenticity is about trust.

Think of Great Britain's two duchesses, Catherine and Meghan. Both are women in their thirties, thrust into a position that they weren't trained for, and each has their different passions, backgrounds and talents. But what unites them is how they have stuck to their individual beliefs and values, promoting causes including mental health and women's rights – two subjects that would have been unthinkable for royalty to discuss even ten years ago – and kept their own uniqueness within the mega-brand that is the royal family. Both women are rightly praised for their authenticity.

To take that back to the business world, there used to be the assumption that to be the boss you had to act like a man, and adopt a similar way of dressing, communication style, perhaps even values. But that's just not true. We now see the value in diversity of thought and ideas. Staying true to yourself and leading authentically is paramount – and in chapter nine you'll read more about how staying true to herself was key to Oprah Winfrey's enormous success.

One of the hardest things I found, however, was maintaining authenticity when you're the only woman at the top. I'm a real chameleon and find it easy to change my style depending on who I am talking to, which makes me a good leader. But in the past I have found it can be a challenge to be myself when surrounded by men. As Beatriz Acevedo mentioned earlier, you have to remember that some of your value comes from your difference.

Professionalism

There's a caveat to authenticity: in my view authenticity is important, but not at the cost of professionalism, by which I mean acting in a way appropriate for the job. For me, an example of being professional is going for an after-work drink with colleagues, but just one; never being the last to leave the bar. Where I've seen this go wrong is when people think bringing their whole selves to work means behaving at work in the same way they would at a bar with friends. Being a loud joker might make colleagues like you but is unlikely to be appropriate in a boardroom or when dealing with a difficult human resources issue. I have always had an open leadership style. I try to be approachable and relatable but that doesn't mean I'm everyone's friend or that I want to hear the ins and outs of their personal lives, or that I share my own.

Sandy Nunez, coordinating producer of *SportsCenter* in LA, has her own warning about maintaining professionalism at all times. 'I was working at ABC News as a producer for 10 years and the deputy bureau chief job came up. I thought I was perfect for it. I interviewed with the bureau chief who I'd worked with in Israel and knew very well and it was very conversational. That was a really big mistake on my part because I did not treat the interview as formally as I should have and I'm fairly certain that I lost the job because I didn't give it the respect and formality that it really deserved. So, I would always say keep everything very professional.'

How you dress

We've focused on the way you talk, but let's not forget how you look. Michelle Obama acknowledges this about her eight-year stint as First Lady: 'Optics governed more or less everything in the political world and I factored this into every outfit.' Similarly, Angela Merkel has said that despite being Chancellor of Germany for 13 years, if a man wears the same dark suit for three months it goes unnoticed; if she wears the same blazer a few times over a couple of weeks, she gets letters in the post. Just as in politics, visuals matter in business, too. As trite as it might sound, studies prove that it's how we look that goes to forming people's first impression of us. Princeton psychologists Janine Willis and Alexander Todorov say that, in fact, it takes as little as a tenth of a second to judge someone. However beautifully crafted your pitch might be, your general appearance is always going to speak first.

The advice applies equally to men as it does to women, and it's nothing new. In fact Polonius had sage advice for his son Laertes when he was heading off to Paris in *Hamlet*: 'The apparel oft proclaims the man.' And whether it's in the Danish court or in the boardroom, his advice is pertinent: you have to be aware of the clothes you're wearing and dress appropriately for the occasion. It's about flexing your style to be advantageous to the situation or your personal brand. If, for example, you're a creative director addressing an audience at Cannes, you need to dress accordingly, but if you're going into a room full of VCs and want to be taken seriously then you might have to think in a different way about your wardrobe choices. You have to choose if it's more important to express your personality or let that fade into the background while your business nous does the talking.

It changes as you do. Elizabeth Uviebiné says that her recent success has given her the confidence to dress in a different manner that speaks more to her personal style.

'I recently was on a panel at a marketing conference, and I wore a long, high-waisted skirt, a crop top, blazer and heels. I looked down at my outfit – which I loved – and thought that I wouldn't have had the confidence to wear that when I was here two years ago; I would have dressed more conservatively as I would have been worried about how people perceived me. Of course, things had changed, I was on the panel instead of being in the audience, and I'd just published a book.'

Similarly, my personal style has changed since stepping down as CEO. Partly it's because I work in a different world where, as the co-founder of a business, I'm allowed to be more myself than when I was representing a big corporation. I don't dress down; in fact, I'm probably a bit more glam now because of the number of events we host and speak at. But I don't need the power suit anymore.

What's interesting is how clothes can make you feel and act, too. A paper in *Social Psychological and Personality Science* described the outcome of a study in which participants were asked to change into formal or casual clothing before completing a series of cognitive tests. Researchers found that when the subjects were wearing formal business clothes it increased their abstract thinking, essential for long-term strategising.

Meanwhile, for a separate paper in the *Journal of Experimental Psychology*, subjects were asked to dress informally or formally and then negotiate a deal with a partner. Those who dressed up won the deal. Debbie, who is always immaculately dressed, says she doesn't feel in the right armour if she's in jeans or flat shoes at work; and let me tell you, she's an amazing negotiator.

Curating your online world

It's not just the real world where we have to make a good first impression. We have so many ways of putting ourselves out there online – including updating social media accounts, writing killer LinkedIn profiles, creating and maintaining websites, podcasts, blogs … it could be a full-time job in itself. But your online profile is a very clear, very instant representation of your personal brand, and something that work contacts are bound to check out before meeting you in the flesh.

Emma Gannon, writer, broadcaster, lecturer, bestselling author and host of blockbuster podcast *CTRL ALT DELETE*, is passionate about teaching people how to curate their online space, having benefited from the opportunities her own afforded her. 'Building a good reputation in your working life is important, and now that most of our lives are spent online, it matters what people see when they type our names into Google,' she says. She suggests opening up an incognito window on your web browser and typing in your name to see what pops up. Check the image search, too. That's what everyone else sees when they Google you. Do you like what you see? If not, change that, fast. Be mindful to be assertive in your online communications, as well as your real-world ones, too.

Marc W. Halpert is a LinkedIn trainer who advises executives on how to promote themselves online. He agrees that we should take the time to keep up to date with our online presence: 'We are all in beta – in our careers, building our businesses, in adopting new technology, and thus, in our brand management. We're always in the process of changing. That means, of course, that we must keep our outward personal brand marketing up to date and relevant, never stale or uninteresting, reflecting the current state of our personal development as professionals, however that may morph.'

How to clean up your LinkedIn profile

A LinkedIn profile is pretty essential in business, and Marc Halpert has some practical tips for cleaning up, or writing, your profile – because remember, you're in charge of what people see about you:

'Decide if you need to update your headshot photo, and think, do I look professional, yet approachable? Remember: it follows you all over LinkedIn (and the internet).' He advises a new headshot every three to five years.

'Does your headline succinctly describe why you do what you do, not blandly list your title and company name? In today's world, you only have the mere 120-character headline to make an immediate electronic impression.'

'Think of your *Summary* section as your elevator pitch: it's a high-level snapshot of where you learned your skills, who you are today, and your goals. In your *Experience* section, make sure it reflects the breadth of what you bring daily to the proverbial table. Describe the key values you learned in each position and how you cultivated your skills. Talk about successes, as this section should complement the other sections.

'Be very specific about your skills: "Marketing" is not a skill per se – "social media marketing analytics" is a more exact skill, as is "integrated marketing analysis".'

If you don't already have a LinkedIn account, then use this as a nudge to set one up.

Building your buzz

With all that noise online, and the frantic pace of our work and home lives, you have to shout out loudly about yourself and your achievements. In fact, your personal brand relies on you doing so, as Professor Jean-Noël Kapferer says in *(Re)Inventing the Brand*: 'A brand's strength is built upon its determination to promote its own distinctive values and mission.'

It can feel embarrassing to do, because as women we're culturally taught to be modest and downplay our achievements. But research from London Business School shows that one big difference between men and women at work is their attitude to boasting. The study found that successful women often cite luck as the reason behind their corporate victories; a man in the same position will brag about his achievements. It's a double whammy if you're British and a woman: British society doesn't – or used not to – encourage boastfulness.

Things are changing as we get more global. In the world of work where it's hard to measure one employee against another – if you ever glance at a pile of graduate CVs you'll see that lots of people get top grades at university and all undertake extra-curricular activities – it's really important to blow your own trumpet. You are your own best PR person, your own social media executive and the person best placed to give your sales pitch, whether that's for your product, or yourself.

'Speak up about your achievements,' says Tracy De Groose, executive chair of Newsworks, the marketing body for UK newspapers. 'On the whole, we're not good enough at merchandising our successes. We don't do it because we're trying to be modest – but we've got to think about how we sell ourselves, because we're selling opportunities for all women.' It's a great point. If you're worried about bragging, then reframe it. When I worked in a corporation, I was great at championing my team and my brands, but I have found it harder when striking out on my own. You have to continue to promote other women, and ask them to do the same for you in return, but you've also got to force yourself to sing your own praises – it's a way to get noticed and promoted. And for that, your personal brand is something to use as your battle shield.

CASE STUDY: KELLY HOPPEN MBE, INTERIOR DESIGNER, AUTHOR AND FOUNDER OF KELLY HOPPEN LONDON

Aged 16, Kelly Hoppen, who had a passion for design, was given the chance to design a family friend's kitchen. It kick-started the award-winning career of one of the best-known and influential interior designers. Since then, Kelly has designed many of the world's most desirable homes, yachts, jets and hotels, with celebrity clients including her good friends David and Victoria Beckham, whose LA home she designed and executed in six weeks.

She is very clear that having a strong personal brand has been key to her success. 'My brand *IS* me,' she says. You can instantly recognise a Kelly Hoppen-designed interior from its clean lines, neutral tones and luxury, her USPs. 'The most important elements of my style are harmony, neutral palettes and global fusion,' she says. 'I've always been influenced by Eastern design philosophies and principles, and I quickly became known for my signature East meets West aesthetic. My USP was organic from day one, creating homes for people to live in, the experience being key.'

It's a winning formula that has made her fantastically successful and in constant demand, and has allowed her to branch out from straight design services, which she still does, to authoring books, opening an e-commerce shop and appearing as a judge on the television programme *Dragons' Den*. Authenticity is at the heart of what she does and has been crucial in a career that has spanned decades and survived fluctuating fashions. 'You need to have a clear focus from the outset,' she says. 'Times change and the needs of people change, and to be successful your brand needs to change with the needs of people, but throughout transition, it needs to always remain authentic and true to itself.'

She says that she struggled with written communication at school because of dyslexia, so instead communicates 'visually, the old-fashioned way, by showing people my work' and creating a network of clients. 'Every job I did was successful, and the word spread. It was a new style that had not previously existed, so I think that helped to establish the Kelly Hoppen look and, in turn, my brand.'

CHAPTER RECAP: Personal Brand

Your personal brand is the key part of your business toolkit. It's as essential to getting that top job as it is to getting investment for a product. We all know good businesses that have done brilliantly or failed dismally because of their branding, and it's the same with you. Make sure you get yours right.

Self-awareness and USPs: To understand your personal brand you need to have good self-awareness and use that – building on your strengths and motivations established in chapters one and two – to work out your USPs. Remember to be specific. That's how you will stand out from the crowd.

Communication style: Women can have a tendency to be passive communicators, but we should aim for an assertive communication style. That means being direct, open, honest and confident in your delivery, while employing empathy and self-awareness to keep your audience and team on the journey with you.

Authenticity and consistency: Being true to your core values is really prized, because it encourages a level of trust. People know who you are and what to expect. It leads on to a great foundation for building up networks, especially if you're consistent in your message and your dealings with people. People and institutions know they can rely on you.

Dress: How we present ourselves to the external world extends to the clothes we wear. Studies show that not only does the way we dress affect how we feel and how we perform, but it affects how people judge us – often within a few seconds. It's really important to dress the part and adopt your battle armour so that you can then focus on your core message.

Online: It's not just the real world where we have to make a good first impression, it's online, too. In fact, that might be the first place people look for us. We are all searchable, so be sure that your digital footprint is one that you are happy with. If it's not, change it, now.

WORKSHEET: IDENTIFYING YOUR PERSONAL BRAND

Anna's personal brand is: she's warm, direct and a fast decision maker, but with inner steel. Now that you've read through this chapter and seen how others define their brand, it's time to consider the elements that make up yours.

Being honest with yourself, and perhaps asking your sisterhood for help, list five USPs. For example, are you good at seeing a problem from different angles? Are you good at communicating a message clearly? Are you focused and precise? A creative thinker who can see opportunities in the most unlikely places?

1 _____
2 _____
3 _____
4 _____
5 _____

Which are the three that you feel are most important to you at work? Condense this down into a sentence:

My personal brand is that I'm _____,
_____ and _____

This statement is something you can remind yourself of when you're going into business battle.

CHAPTER SIX

Your Business Toolkit

'A confident person – knowing and believing in her identity – carries tools, not weapons'

Amy Cuddy

Debbie

When I founded my first company in my mid twenties, we grew exponentially in the first year of the business, but the costs were out of control. Our office was opposite the luxury hotel Claridge's, which was basically our canteen and my team were in there the whole time. I got to the end of the first year and realised, 'Hang on, we've billed £3 million in sales, but I've only made £60k, how has this happened?' There's nothing like experience to teach you that you need to get a very firm grip on your numbers. Especially when it's your money. Let's say I learned quickly.

One of the things women often feel underconfident around is finance; we hear and see that a lot through talking to our members and also when hearing from businesses that want investment from us. But understanding the dynamics of your business isn't the same as 'being good at maths'. It's about really understanding what makes someone buy your product or service and being totally comfortable with the business basics. As Jack Lew, who served as Secretary to the Treasury under President Obama, explained, 'The budget is not just a collection of numbers, but an expression of our values and aspirations.' The same applies to business. Your finances show what you are and how you can grow.

It's obviously essential to have a handle on your numbers if you've got your own business; the path to entrepreneurial glory is littered with those who just didn't have a grip on their stats. Nasty Gal is an interesting example here. This is the clothing business that Sophia Amoruso built up from her bedroom in San Francisco into a brand that was generating $300 million in sales and saw her listed in Forbes' list of America's self-made millionaires. But later that same year, the business filed for bankruptcy. The reason? Sophia recently said it was because she took her eyes off the numbers and the overall direction of the business, assuming that those she'd hired would take care of the details. It's a lesson we can all learn. Of course, you have to trust your colleagues and team around you to do their job, but that's not a substitute for knowing what's going on yourself.

Anna and I always talk about how you need to be willing to run after a £5 note as it flutters down the street – and it's important to be able to chase it around your bank statements, too. Many of my businesses have been down to the last £1,000 in their accounts before a vital round of funding, so I got into the habit of checking my business bank balance every day. It's something I still do today.

Knowing about key business levers of the corporation you work in, outside your specific role, is equally important if you want to progress through the ranks in an organisation, too. You've got to know how a business ticks and understand the potential for scale.

Melanie Whelan, CEO of SoulCycle, says that her number one tip for women who want to advance is to understand the P&L – she explains more at the end of the chapter. Even if you've got no interest in being the finance woman, or the sales whizz, *Slay in Your Lane* author Elizabeth Uviebiné says, 'It's important to be open to new ideas and skills that aren't necessarily in your day job. I think a lot of the time we see defined barriers to roles, and that's limiting. But ultimately not being incredible at managing spreadsheets isn't what will hold you back.' What will stunt your career growth, she says, is 'not being able to ask for help'. We couldn't agree more.

Just as you've worked on learning about yourself inside out, so you have to do that for the company you work in or lead. A working knowledge of its finances – including financial opportunities – sales and business models are all key areas to get to grips with. If you don't know them, learn now. You might have to do this at any part of your career. Dame Marjorie Scardino remembers being appointed as CEO of the publishing giant Pearson and having 'to scurry away after the meeting and check the difference between buy side and sell side … I thought, God, what have I got myself into?' You'll read more about her success in that job in chapter nine, but what her experience shows is that all those figures and terms can be learned, and your work sisterhood can help you plug the gaps.

Once you've got a total snapshot of your business it will help you feel invincible in any upcoming situation. It means you can step into meetings with senior people within your organisation – or even those fleeting moments such as in the queue for the coffee – and feel confident that you can contribute meaningfully. A little bit of knowledge can help you shine.

This chapter is a really practical workbook where we explain the basics, including how to interpret financial statements. Some aspects you may well be familiar with, others might be ringing distant bells, or be totally new. Use this as a springboard to go off and dig deeper into your own business because, to succeed, you need to tool up and keep up to date. No excuses.

What you'll learn in this chapter:

- How to understand your finances
- The five key financial numbers to know
- Why you need a business model
- The importance of a sales strategy
- How your business toolkit is vital to your success

Success is a numbers game

If someone comes in to pitch their business to Anna and I, and says, 'I don't really do the numbers,' then that's the end of the conversation. It's amazing how many people don't want to talk about finance, even in an investment meeting – they want to talk about the softer stuff, the reason behind the business and their vision for world domination. But without the numbers, and knowing and understanding the story they tell, a business and its leader are not backable. That's not to say you have to know everything; some things you can't know, such as future market forces, for instance. It is perfectly OK to say, 'This is what we know at the moment and this is the assumption.' But you have to be upfront about the gaps in your knowledge, so that it doesn't look like sloppy homework.

Perhaps it sounds grubby and unromantic to some, but money really is at the heart of all business. Everything costs money in our daily lives and we understand that. Yet for some reason it's an area that many people, and especially women, fear when it comes to business. Not for me, and not for CEO Anastasia Soare either, who says, 'I grew up in a family where women were the financiers, they held the finances. It never occurred to me that women wouldn't be good with finances; every woman could be savvy with her money.'

Really, it's quite simple: the two critical areas you need to understand about the business are how the business makes money and what drives profitability. It's literally: 'Something costs this, I sell it for that, do I have a profit at the end of it? How can I make more?' It's as simple as that and you need to know it, both as a founder and as an exec.

Olivia Wollenberg is the founder of her healthy snack brand Livia's Kitchen, which makes healthy, gluten-free, vegan sweet treats which are stocked in Selfridges, Whole Foods and Harvey Nichols, as well as leading supermarkets. She launched her business in 2015 and says, as a young founder with no previous business experience, she made crucial mistakes around not knowing her numbers.

'I definitely made big mistakes in the early days because I was not as on top of the numbers as I should have been,' she admits. 'My very first product, which I manufactured myself in my parents' kitchen, I only factored in the ingredient and packaging costs and did not leave any room for labour and distribution. When I then looked to outsource production and distribution of this product, we would have been making a negative margin if I'd stuck to the same recipe and other fixed costs. It was a huge learning curve moment.' It's a simple business figure – the gross margin (see below) – in which she would go on to become expert.

Olivia says she now has a very experienced commercial director and head of finance who handle the finances of the business day-to-day. But, she adds, 'I am always very close to the numbers, though, so that I can track our progress.' Her financial savvy has paid off. In the last two years, her turnover has increased by 475 per cent, and in the last year the number of stores she is listed in has increased by 389 per cent. Anyone can understand that that signals success, with hopefully more to come.

Four key financial terms to know

Financial terms only sound tricky to those who aren't used to reading them. Once you realise that they are just code to understanding what's going on with the health of your business, they become demystified. Work out how to read them and the key terminology you need to use, and you'll never feel underconfident around finances again.

1. Profit and Loss

The profit and loss (or P&L or income statement) is a measure of financial performance, providing a view of your company's income and expenditure over a specified period. Your P&L will summarise sales and, after deduction of your company's cost of sales, will show your gross margin, such as the profit generated from activity directly attributable to the creation, manufacture and distribution of your product. From your gross margin you will deduct your administrative expenses to derive net profit. By keeping an eye on gross profit and gross profit margin you can ensure that the direct cost of producing goods is in line with your expectation, and by keeping close control on net profit you can ensure that your bottom line is not being eroded by spiralling administrative costs.

2. Balance sheet

The balance sheet provides a snapshot at any given moment of what the business owns and what the business owes – right now. This statement will summarise the value of the business's assets (things like land, buildings, equipment, investments, inventory, debtors and cash) and will deduct its liabilities (loans, overdrafts, mortgages, debt owed to suppliers) to determine the overall wealth, or net assets, of the business.

3. Equity versus debt

These important terms describe the ways in which you can finance your business. Simply put, equity is cash taken from individuals (such as angel investors) or institutions (such as venture capital firms) who invest in the business expecting a return on their capital either by dividend or future share sale. Debt represents cash taken from a lender who expects a return on their capital by way of regular interest payments and repayment of capital. Both are important means of growing a business, but the fundamental difference is that an equity investor will take an ownership stake in your business, and therefore has a say in how it operates, whereas a lender of debt finance will not. Neither is 'better' than the other, but it is important to understand and critically assess each option as you look to scale your business.

4. Cash flow

The old adage 'cash is king' remains as relevant as ever – a business needs sufficient cash to be able to meet its debts as they fall due or it will become insolvent – which is game over. The cash flow forecast is a tool that will enable you to project your cash inflows and outgoings into the future to ensure that you don't fall short.

Talking to investors

I have spent my whole career trying to persuade rooms full of men to invest in my businesses, and I know from experience that women have to fight harder to be heard and to get the cash. Globally, only 10 per cent of venture capital funds went to female founders between 2010 and 2015, and the situation is actually getting worse, with only 2.7 per cent of venture capital funding in 2016 going to female-led businesses in the UK, and slightly less in the US.

There are myriad reasons why this is the case: historically men have had control of money and the world of finance is structured around male power. Most often, those investors are male. 'There can be an unconscious bias, particularly for women, when you're raising money, if you don't get your numbers right, or are not in control of them, people may assume that you don't know them. You have to be all over it,' Caroline Plumb, serial entrepreneur and founder and CEO of fintech start-up Fluidly, says.

When I'm acting as an angel investor, I find all too often that women tend to under-pitch their business, because they don't focus enough on how to 'sell the dream' to investors. I had a meeting with a young founder who was, by all markers of success, doing very well. But she came into the meeting very apologetically and spent a long time telling her personal story behind the business. I want to hear her motivations as part of the business story, of course, but it's worth about one minute of my time. What I want to hone in on is the figures: the cost of the product, the price point, projected sales, historical data and opportunities for growth. Men do that. They come in armed with stats, as Anna always has done, too. When she went in to negotiate budget numbers for Hearst, she would have to know the details on all the profit and loss sheets for all 25 businesses in her portfolio because she knew that she would be asked about an obscure number on one P&L sheet. She prepped like it was an exam, spending the weekend before going through spreadsheets and making it her business to know every single number, because that was her armour going into the meeting.

What's at the heart of these meetings? 'Investors are going to want to know how they can make money – you not only have to show a passion for your product, but a passion for your business, and demonstrate that you are excited and knowledgeable about how your business will make money,' Alice Bentinck, co-founder of Entrepreneur First, the business builder and start-up accelerator based in London and Singapore, says. It includes how much you will charge for your product, who you're going to sell it to, how you'll sell it, how much it costs to make product, the cost of acquiring customers (CAC) versus the lifetime value of your customer (LTV).

When it's a female investor behind the desk, then they are more likely to support female businesses, according to a report by the Overland Park-based Angel Capital Association. But, frustratingly, female angels are in the minority: only 14 per cent in the UK according to a 2015 report and a slightly healthier 22 per cent in the US. It's something we're trying to address with AllBright; we want to increase the amount of funding to female businesses and so we have a monthly Pitch Day, where we invite female-founded businesses to present to our network of experienced angel investors, high-net-worth individuals and business leaders. It's a start.

Here's a final stat for you to quote: according to research, women are a better business bet. Research by the global managing consultancy company BCG found that businesses founded by women ultimately delivered higher revenue – more than twice as much per dollar invested. We just need to be better at presenting ourselves as a sure thing. Get your numbers sorted now, and we'll show you how to negotiate that deal in chapter ten.

A Guide to Understanding Financial Statements

If you can read a financial statement, you give yourself an instant success boost. There are a number of 'ratios' which essentially allow you to read between the lines.

Below are some of the most common ratios and how you work them out.

RATIOS TO HELP YOU UNDERSTAND PROFITABILITY

GROSS PROFIT PERCENTAGE

Gross profit divided by turnover: $\dfrac{\text{Gross Profit}}{\text{Turnover}}$

NET PROFIT PERCENTAGE

Profit for the financial year divided by turnover:

$$\frac{\text{Profit for the financial year}}{\text{Turnover}}$$

RETURN ON CAPITAL EMPLOYED

Profit before tax and interest divided by total assets less current liabilities:

$$\frac{\text{Profit before tax and interest}}{\text{(Total assets} - \text{Current liabilities)}}$$

RATIOS TO HELP YOU UNDERSTAND LIQUIDITY

ACID TEST

Current assets less stock divided by current liabilities:

$$\frac{\text{(Current assets} - \text{Stock)}}{\text{Current liabilities}}$$

CURRENT RATIO
Current assets divided by current liabilities:

$$\frac{\text{Current assets}}{\text{Current liabilities}}$$

Business model

If you're in a big corporation, it's useful to know or work out the company business model because it serves as a snapshot of that business. There's a huge variation in business models, depending on the type of product or service you sell. As Alice Bentinck explains: 'You look at the product – whether its ephemeral like a service, or physical, like a packet of crisps – and work out how much you're selling the product for, how much it costs to sell, including your route to market, such as a retailer or your own website, and look at the other costs involved, from people, to distribution, to advertising and marketing.'

It's not unusual not to know all these details. I didn't with Love Home Swap. It started out as a business that was: one person lives in Paris, another lives in Sydney and they swap homes. We did that for about three years. But we realised that a straight swap was impractical for lots of people, so we built up a swapping currency. Even the AllBright business model is something different now to when we started, but you don't know until you start trying.

Alice, who is an expert at this, admits that she and her co-founder struggled with their business model when they started out in 2011: 'What we were doing hadn't been done before, so there wasn't a clear way to charge our customers. When we tried to grow, we realised that without a business model we couldn't scale.' Since then, they've nailed it. Not only have they helped build nearly 150 businesses, but last year they received funding of $12.4 million, proving that once you get the basics sorted, it will really help with your future growth.

Guide to terminology

CAC – cost of acquiring customers: how much it costs to get someone to buy your product, for instance marketing costs or promotional offers.

LTV – Lifetime value of your customer: how much money you can expect to make from your customer in the long term.

Sales strategy

Whether you work as an executive in a corporation or you're the CEO, your company's ultimate responsibility is to deliver a profit to its shareholders. If you make yourself interested in where commercial opportunities might lie, then you've got a fast track to the top.

The people we've seen do really well are those who understand the commercial realities of their business, regardless of their position in the company. You might be the restaurant manager, but if you can spot that a certain coffee is flying out of the door and work out why, then you'll be delivering profit for your business and you'll be noticed.

Understanding a business's sales strategy is key, and to do this, you need to understand your customer. It's important to think about why your offer is important to them: are you solving a problem or helping them aspire to something incredible? You then need to build a detailed picture of what your customer looks like in terms of where they live, what their interests are, what's important to them. As Atticus says to Scout in *To Kill a Mockingbird*, 'You never really understand a person until you consider things from his point of view ... until you climb in his skin and walk around in it.' That's what you need to do with your customer.

'Building valuable insight about your customer and their behaviours will help you deliver a more personalised experience where your product or service can really resonate,' says Dalia Nightingale, business growth advisor at DDN Consulting. 'It's critical to do your market research, and understand the size of the market, how many potential customers you could be targeting, so you know the real size of the opportunity for your business. Additionally, keeping on top of your competitors, what they are doing and how they are positioning themselves in comparison, will help you differentiate and develop both your product and killer sales messaging.'

It's something you need to keep an eye on. Cassandra Stavrou, co-founder of Propercorn, tells this cautionary tale: 'We launched a new product, Crunch Corn, which was half popped popcorn. We were trying to establish a whole new category of snacks, and we just didn't get the strategy right. Quite simply it didn't sell well, and we had to take the painful decision to take the product off the shelves.' It really highlights the importance of understanding the sales strategy inside out.

CASE STUDY: MELANIE WHELAN, CEO SOULCYCLE

Melanie Whelan, CEO of SoulCycle, the cult American spinning studio that transformed boutique fitness, says her top tip for women who want to scale the corporate ladder is to put themselves in charge of a company's P&L. It obviously worked for her: Melanie has been named in Fortune's 40 Under 40, Crain's New York 40 Under 40, and Fast Company's Most Creative People in Business.

'Understanding the purpose of the business, its economic model and how to inspire and galvanise the people around you to make it happen is so important,' she says. 'The sooner you can truly understand the levers of the business, the sooner you can make more meaningful contributions to your team and to your company. Of course, there are many great careers that don't directly involve driving a P&L, but I will say that once you understand how a company makes top-line revenue and the different variables and expenses that drive it, you put yourself in a position to be a leader. You have context on how decisions get made and their impact. For me, this was transformative for my career.'

Indeed, after studying engineering and economics at the Ivy League Brown University, Melanie had a range of jobs in business development, from leadership positions with Virgin Management, vice president of business development at Equinox and COO of SoulCycle before being appointed to the top job in 2015. Under her leadership, the brand has grown to more than 90 studios in the US and Canada, and this year, to London.

But she says that one of her early jobs, working for a single yoga studio in New York, was where she developed her business nous. 'Though it started as a single studio business, what I've learned now is that the principles and the discipline behind the P&L of that business are no different than the much larger one that we operate today. Vision can only be realised through the lens of execution, which comes down to building and driving the economic model of the business. There's just so much empowerment in truly understanding the P&L. It really allows you to have a bigger impact on your teams and company.'

She advises that even if you're not the money woman in your organisation, knowing your business numbers, as well as the business model and sales strategies, is still key to success. 'Anyone should have context on their work,' she says. 'Ultimately, as a leader in a business, what you spend your days focused on and prioritising should always be contextualised in the business model of the company. The best way to advance in any career is to add value beyond the role you're in. I've always tried to not only do what's asked or required, but go one step further. Connect the dots beyond your role – that's where the impact lies.'

CHAPTER RECAP: Your Business Toolkit

There are key tools that all businesses use. You've got to know how a business ticks and understand the potential for scale in order to grow and succeed. Some people are put off by the terminology, but it's just another language to master. Once you have, you'll be fluent in business speak and it will add to your growing career confidence. But don't be afraid to reach out to your work sisterhood to ask for help with knowledge gaps, if you need it.

Know your numbers: Finance is at the heart of all businesses: it's what keeps them alive and what enables growth. Knowing a set of financial numbers is not the same as being good or bad at maths, so don't be put off from the start. There is some key terminology to learn, and from there, it's easy.

Four financial terms you need to know: If you want to demystify a budget meeting, learn some key terms, and what the numbers on the spreadsheet actually represent.

Talking to investors: Statistics show that women are at a disadvantage when it comes to attracting investment. There are some cultural and societal forces at play here, but we can boost our presentations by making sure we stick to stats, not stories.

Financial statements: There are a number of 'ratios' that allow you to read between the lines and understand certain things about your business. Once you can read a financial statement with ease, you know at a glance what is going on with a company.

Business model: Whether you're in a big corporation or a founder, it's useful to know or work out the business model because it serves as a snapshot of that company. It includes detail on how much you will charge for your product, who you're going to sell it to, how you'll sell it, how much it costs to make the product, the cost of acquiring customers (CAC) versus the lifetime value of your customer (LTV).

Sales strategy: Sales are – largely – where businesses make their money. By understanding a sales strategy and where the opportunities are, you'll propel yourself to the top.

WORKSHEET: KNOWING YOUR NUMBERS

It's so crucial that you understand what's going on in your business, whether you're a founder or if you're employed in a bigger company, because that is key to spotting opportunities. We said there are four key financial terms to learn, do you know what they mean in relation to your workplace? Go through them now and find out – and if you don't know, ask someone fill in the gaps with you.

1 _____

_____

2 _____

_____

3 _____

_____

4 _____

_____

CHAPTER SEVEN

The Balancing Act

'Don't confuse having a career with having a life'

Hillary Rodham Clinton

Anna

I know what it's like to feel as if you have to give everything either to work, or to your family. When I was working at my most manic in senior roles in corporations, I gave all my energy to my kids and the job, and totally neglected my own wellbeing. It's so tempting, especially when you love what you do, to squeeze in another late night or early start. As a result, I had loads of horrible illnesses from pneumonia to quinsy. It was totally debilitating, and no job is worth being that ill.

I'm not alone, of course. The most common excuse we all make not to dedicate time to wellness is that we're too busy. But as up to 80 per cent of all GP consultations are thought to be somehow related to stress, it makes sense to nurture our wellness before it turns into a bigger problem. A recent study found that women are more likely to experience 'burnout' in whatever guise that might take than men, because men are better at taking breaks throughout the day. Men are 25 per cent more likely to go off for personal activities, 7 per cent more likely to take a walk, 5 per cent more likely to go out for lunch and 35 per cent more likely to take breaks 'just to relax'. Having seen the effect that overwork can have on my health, these days I'm so much better at speaking up when I'm not feeling in peak condition, because frankly I don't have time *not to* prioritise wellness.

Factored into this is the question of work–life balance, which is often talked about and if we're not careful can feel like another thing we fail at. It's so tricky because the nature of work has changed. For Debbie and I, what we do is a passion as well as a livelihood, and it's an important part of our identity, so we like to think about integrating work as part of our lives. I have children – as does Debbie, along with many of the women in our club and the inspirational business-women mentioned in these pages – and I think it's important that our children have an understanding of our work. We both bring them to our AllBright clubs – Debbie's kids had birthday parties in our first club – and they know what our business is. My daughter says that women can do anything, because she understands the AllBright mission and she's seen what we do. Debbie and I are more than business partners, we are friends and as well as working together, we also choose to spend social time together.

'How do you manage it all?' is definitely one of the more regular questions we face. We get asked it in almost every press interview we do – I'm sure a man in our position never does. But the truth is, it's a balancing act.

The concept of balancing the different areas of your life is important. We've found that it's crucial to our members too, with 56 per cent of respondents within the AllBright community saying a balanced life is critical to feeling success-ful, accomplished and happy. That's huge. But it takes some thought. You need to have strategies and boundaries in place to help keep everything in check. It's the oxygen mask metaphor – if you take care of yourself, you've got more to give.

What you'll learn in this chapter:

- To assess your boundaries, and prioritise
- To lean on your support network
- To incorporate wellness in your business journey
- The importance of taking care of your mental health
- How to invest in yourself

How to achieve balance

Debbie and I feel privileged to be able to go into our office every day and be surrounded by the inspiring women who work with us. There should be no shame in admitting you love your work – that's a great thing. But there are still days when, despite this, I can feel totally drained of energy or distracted with things going on in my personal life. That's when I realise that I have to redress the balance – perhaps take an afternoon off, or at least go for a walk at lunch time to get some air and a bit of headspace. Does it mean I've found balance? Not really, but it's making those daily tweaks which help me feel a bit more in tune.

Balance means different things to everyone. It might mean getting back to do the school pickup and then getting the work done after bath time; maybe it's getting up early to train for a triathlon, or making sure to spend evenings with friends and family or on a favourite hobby. 'The balancing act shouldn't be a long-term goal, it's a daily thing that you try to keep in check, but it will never be right,' says Nicola Elliott, founder of the bestselling UK wellness brand Neom Organics. 'You've got to make your peace with that, because it's not something that you'll crack.'

Accepting you can't do it all

This means you have to accept that you will drop a few balls – and it's up to you to decide which are the least important.

'One of the hardest lessons for me to learn was that striving for perfection was unrealistic and actually counterproductive,' says Paula Kaplan, executive vice president, talent and development at Viacom Digital Studios. 'You simply cannot be 100 per cent at all things, at all times, to all people. Accepting this has opened me up to more possibility, more creativity and deeper relationships. Trusting yourself to be the best you are capable of being at any moment is what is key. Then you must use that trust to leverage your expertise and build your success.'

That means not obsessing over trying to do too much at the expense of spreading yourself too thin. Nicola agrees: 'You've got to think, is the business that much better if you get out one more product or marketing campaign? If we're getting seven out of ten things done here, that's great.'

Clare Johnston, founder of the Up Group executive recruitment consultancy, says that accepting you can't do it all helps your business grow too: 'I wore multiple hats at the start when I was founding my business and tried to kid myself that I could do it all and work more hours in the day. But it slows growth. You have to be able to hand "your baby" over to other people.' It can be hard, but as well as helping you, it also empowers others in your team.

Prioritising

So, how do you prioritise? When she was First Lady of the United States, Michelle Obama said: 'If you don't take control over your time and your life, other people will gobble it up.' It's true even if you don't have national responsibilities: you have to jump in first and prioritise what's important to you, before anyone else demands your time. I totally relate to that, as there have been periods in my career when I've let the many demands on my diary totally take over and have felt close to burnout with not a minute to myself or for my needs. Zena Everett is one of the UK's leading careers experts and an executive coach on the University of Oxford Saïd Business School's global executive MBA programme: 'The first thing I suggest is, at the start of every day, to think about the three things that you need to move your business forward,' she says. 'It's not rocket science, but it takes you out of the routine stuff and on to the strategic stuff.' That includes thinking about the conversations you need to have, the relationships you need to build and the dreams you need space to dream. 'If you manage to do those three things, then you've had a great day.' Perhaps you include things you need on a personal level, too.

Lots of CEOs swear by scheduling. Zena says that you need to get your diary out – ideally on a Friday afternoon when your productivity might be waning – and look for 90-minute gaps in your schedule the following week to book in time to do priority tasks.

If we don't plan this time, Zena says, we are in danger of derailing ourselves with other tasks. 'Women in particular can feel guilty when we're doing selfish working, the stuff for our own career. We think, "Why aren't I getting on with the jobs that I really need to do?", or "Why am I doing this instead of spending more time with my direct reports?" Schedule time for the deep stuff, and also short one-to-ones with reports or family – it helps you feel less guilty.'

This kind of planning ultimately leaves us feeling more fulfilled. If we're organised, it leaves us less time for the mindless social media scrolling, and gives us a greater sense of satisfaction that we've completed important tasks and are growing our business selves. 'At the end of the day, you can sleep well, knowing you've done as much as possible,' Zena says.

Setting your boundaries

Part of prioritising is figuring out what your boundaries are. Perhaps you set up filters on your email, so that during certain times of day only your boss can contact you. Or perhaps it's that you have to take a lunch break to do a fitness class and get the blood pumping. Debbie's and my boundaries are our kids: if there is a school play at 2.30pm, we're there. They are our absolute priority. But we often work late or are away on overnight trips, and that's the trade-off.

'Finding that divide means that you ultimately have more to give,' says Amisha Ghadiali, wellbeing mentor. 'I know that weekends can be really good for getting work things done,' she adds, 'but it's important to have at least one day a week to switch off from work, perhaps even turning off your email.' We both are quite strict about weekends – even if we do have a few things to work on, we try really hard not to talk about work with family and friends. The reason is quite obvious, but it's one we can forget when we're in the hamster wheel. You have to take care of yourself and keep yourself operating at full capacity so that you can continue to push forward, at work and at home.

Family

How does this work with being a mother? It's hard. We're now having children at older ages than before – in the UK the average age of a first-time mother is 28. In the US, the stats differ according to whether you live in the city or a more rural area, but in New York and San Francisco, the average age is 31 and 32 respectively. It means we're at a key point in our careers when we have children, if we do choose to have them (never mind when babies two or three come along). If what you want is to absorb yourself in motherhood, then totally enjoy that time. I took eight months off with my first child, but kept in touch while I was off, and came back and was promoted. It can be done.

Lynda Gratton, professor of management practice at London Business School, studies women at work, and particularly mothers. The latest research on inequality isn't focused on the differences between men and women, it's about mothers. 'Women's careers can take a back seat when they have children,' she says. 'It's not true of everyone, lots of women do have kids and carry on working. But it's hard to do that, especially if you have more than one.' She says that data shows that if men take paternity leave, they're equally discriminated against. 'So it's not a mother thing, it's a parent thing,' she adds. But as women still tend to do most of the caring, she says that 'men have to step up in terms of their responsibilities' and organisations need to support parents – jointly – better. We now have the option of shared parental leave in the UK, which allows parents to share 50 weeks of leave and 37 weeks of pay after they have a baby. At Hearst, I really encouraged men to take this up, because I feel that dads being more involved as parents is essential to women's equality. But the national take-up is still low, around, 2 per cent. We've made a start, but there's a long way to go before this is normalised.

If you have children, you often find that you have to set up different work structures. Lisa Licht, former chief marketing officer at Live Nation, the American events promoter and venue operator, remembers creating a new structure for herself at a previous company. 'All the women above me at a former company were moms, but they had a lot of help at home with live-in nannies and they were never in a rush to go home. I had always believed in dinner as a family. So I told my bosses that I would be the first one in, and I got in at seven in the morning, but that I would have to be out the door at six. I would then be back online at 8.30 after the kids went to bed.' You have to find what works for you.

The one thing I've found, though, is that it is very hard to go from 'work you' to 'Mummy', just like that. Kids are full of energy and demanding, and need all of you, so you need a switch-off mechanism that's unique to you. I have a long road to walk down to get to my house, and after a trying day I used to visualise actually taking off my 'work cloak'. I would take a few moments to think about what my kids had likely been doing that day and to picture the scene I was about to walk into, so that when I went through the door, I walked in not as a distracted CEO but as Mummy. When Debbie gets home, she takes off her heels, heads straight upstairs to get changed and has five minutes before she comes down and says hello to her kids. It is really useful to have a ritual that you can employ to shift modes.

Support network

The key to keeping your sanity is a support network. When you first return to work, I really advocate finding other new mums in your organisation to help you navigate the early months, because there is an adjustment period where you feel like you are bad at being a mother and bad at work. It's hard.

But you need support at home, too. Women do a double shift: on average, 54 per cent of women do all or most of the household work, compared to 22 per cent of men. This gap grows when couples have children. Women with a partner and children are 5.5 times more likely than their male counterparts to do all or most of the household work. Even when women are primary breadwinners, they do more work at home.

Partner and friends

Aside from your business network, and your children, if you have them, there are other crucial relationships to keep investing in; it's a sisterhood of a different kind. Friendships are vital to our happiness; I've got a gang of friends whom I've known since my first job, on whom I absolutely rely. We are so close that our husbands' nickname for us is 'the cult'. A study suggests that it takes 50 hours before an acquaintance becomes a casual friend; 90 before they become a friend and more than 200 before they become a best friend. These things take time, and you have to keep investing in them to keep the relationships alive and healthy. It's perfectly fine to have a few months off and send your apologies, but at some point you need to connect back in.

Similarly, if you have a partner, you need to be careful to continue to invest in that relationship, too. Jon Moulton, a venture capitalist, conducted his own research and found that CEOs had a higher-than-average divorce rate, while anecdotally the same is said of entrepreneurs, because of the stresses and strains of the job and long, isolating working hours. In a 2013 *New York Times* piece, Erin Callan, the former CFO of Lehman Brothers, wrote: 'Work always came first before my family, friends and marriage – which ended just a few years later.' She reflects that she could have carved out more time for her partner: 'I didn't have to be on my BlackBerry from my first moment in the morning to my last moment at night. I didn't have to eat the majority of my meals at my desk. I didn't have to fly overnight to a meeting in Europe on my birthday. I now believe that I could have made it to a similar place with at least some better version of a personal life.'

However you structure it, it's important to keep tabs on those vital relationships, including making yourself available for others to lean on. You need your entire network in good times and in bad – yours and theirs.

The importance of wellness

Women can be quite bad at prioritising wellness; we have a tendency to look around, check everyone else is OK and soldier on. Debbie and I have both been guilty of that in the past. Luckily, now we have the benefit of being a bit wiser, and we look out for each other.

Eating well

We all know that wellness starts, often, with eating well. No one can concentrate when they're hungry, so don't put yourself on a crazy diet, but instead focus on nutritious wholefoods and snacks such as smoothies, fruit and nuts. Nutritionists often recommend protein with each meal, as it fills us up better than carbs alone, and there are lots of foods that have been shown in scientific studies to increase brain capacity. Green leafy vegetables are rich in brain-healthy nutrients like vitamin K, lutein, folate and beta carotene; berries contain micronutrients called flavonoids, which help women specifically improve their memory, according to a study published in *Annals of Neurology*; while walnuts are thought to improve cognitive function, according to a 2015 study from UCLA.

Don't forget to drink lots of water, too. 'If you're not drinking two or three litres a day your system is dehydrated,' Amisha Ghadiali says. 'Dehydration affects our mood, productivity, bodily functions, everything.'

We know that if we're tired and stressed then it's easy to reach for sugar and caffeine. But while of course everyone should have some treats, we all know that we need to keep an eye on our sugar and alcohol intake, as too much can have disastrous effects on our cortisol levels – our stress hormone – raising them further. 'If you don't look after yourself, you can get into a cycle of going from one cake to the next cake, a cup of coffee to a glass of wine. It's important to step out of that cycle, because that ends up in burnout,' Amisha says.

A good substitute for coffee is hot water with lemon, particularly when we get up in the morning. Most of us think we need a caffeine hit first thing, but studies show that it's not even effective until at least 9am when cortisol, which, among other functions, is responsible for waking you up, stops rising in your blood stream.

Blood and hormone tests

I think it's really important for women, especially as we get older, to get our blood and hormone levels tested. Recently, I was feeling out of whack and Debbie suggested I get tested. The results came back that my vitamin D and iron, which is the most common deficiency for women, were totally depleted. The standard setting for my hormones seems to be a system overloaded with cortisol – the 'fight or flight' hormone that kicks in when we're always fuelled by adrenalin. To compensate, I have to ensure I get plenty of sleep to restore energy reserves (and I am always working on other techniques – like exercise – to bring that cortisol down). It's not enough to only consider our health when we're at death's door. We have to get better at thinking, 'How do I feel, and how do I want to feel?' We need to be fighting fit.

Exercise

Breaking a sweat daily is as important for its mind-boosting qualities as it is for getting your blood pumping. Debbie is an exercise fanatic and boxes every morning by 6am. My version is 20 minutes of Pilates every morning when I wake up. I also walk everywhere. At pace. Before starting my own company, I found it hard to fit in exercise around my job and children. My realisation was that I had to make it part of my daily routine to truly make it a habit.

The nature of modern jobs and work means that we sit down, a lot. Adults of working age in England average about 9.5 hours per day of sedentary time, according to the British Heart Foundation. We already know that sitting for too long is really bad for us: people who spend long periods of time sitting have been found to have higher rates of diabetes and cardiovascular disease, and sitting also has a negative impact on our mental health. The amount we sit, and its effects, has led to the *Harvard Business Review* calling sitting the 'smoking of our generation'. Doing a bit of exercise every day can really help reverse that, and it can be as simple as taking walking meetings, which I find are really useful for squeezing extra catch-ups into a manic day.

For those of us in business, surely the fact that exercise is proven to improve memory and learning capacity is a huge incentive. Researchers at the University of British Columbia found that regular aerobic exercise can boost the size of the hippocampus, the brain area involved in memory and learning. It wasn't even very much exercise; participants got the brain-boosting benefits from walking briskly for one hour, twice a week. I certainly find it helps.

The importance of sleep

I am absolutely crazy about sleep. I need at least seven solid hours a night and once I'm out, I sleep like a log. Debbie's not so lucky, she's a fitful sleeper. I go to bed about 11pm and tend to read digital media on my phone (I know it's bad and that I should really reduce screen time at night, but it works for me). Then I use the notes app on my phone to write down anything on my mind, so that when I close my eyes, I don't have niggling thoughts or to-do lists floating around in my head.

While a lack of sleep used to be a point of pride – think of Margaret Thatcher's famous boast that she only needed four hours a night, or President Trump who claims the same – actually getting enough sleep is now business 101.

Many business leaders now see prioritising sleep as a key responsibility. 'Making a small number of key decisions well is more important than making a large number of decisions,' Amazon CEO Jeff Bezos wrote in the Thrive Journal. 'If you short change your sleep, you might get a couple of extra "productive" hours, but that productivity might be an illusion. When you're talking about decisions and interactions, quality is usually more important than quantity.'

Meanwhile, Arianna Huffington, the self-billed 'sleep evangelist', recently wrote an open letter to entrepreneur Elon Musk, begging him to prioritise his sleep, after he admitted to working 120 hours per week and sleeping on the factory floor. She wrote: 'You're a science and data-driven person. You're obsessed with physics, engineering, with figuring out how things work. So apply that same passion for science not just to your products but to yourself.

People are not machines. For machines – whether of the First or Fourth Industrial Revolution variety – downtime is a bug; for humans, downtime is a feature. The science is clear.'

Most adults need around six to eight hours, according to the National Sleep Foundation, although that's an average, you'll know what you need to feel like a functioning human being.

Mental health

These days, thankfully, mental health is at the top of our wellness – and business – agenda. I'm really sensitive to mental health issues because a number of people close to me have suffered and still suffer from them. Plenty of entrepreneurs and business leaders have detailed their struggles, including Bumble founder Whitney Wolfe Herd. Whitney has spoken about suffering from depression and how, during her dark times, she would read about other successful tech entrepreneurs and see how perfect their lives seemed to be, thinking, 'This will never be me because I have all these problems.' (More from Whitney at the end of chapter eight.)

But she was – and is – by no means alone. Dr Michael Freeman, a clinical professor of psychiatry at UC San Francisco School of Medicine and an entrepreneur himself, surveyed 242 entrepreneurs about their mental health in 2010. He found that nearly half (49 per cent) said that, yes, they had some kind of mental health condition, with depression being the highest reported (30 per cent), and ADHD (29 per cent) and anxiety (27 per cent) not far behind. With the increased discussion and awareness around mental health in more recent years, those percentages may be even higher now.

Psychologists speculate that business leaders and entrepreneurs might even be more vulnerable to mental health problems because of the increased stress of their jobs, and that the higher up in a company you get, the lonelier it can become. It's rarely discussed, but it can be lonely at the top. Even more so if you're a woman and the first one in, there are all kinds of added pressures. It's more important than ever in these situations to reach out for help.

Coping strategies

Whether we have mental health issues or not, stress is a big problem for all of us. We need to develop ways of tackling it by building up support strategies. 'You need to take the time to reflect,' Sarah Wood advises. 'But sometimes knowing when to stop is hard.'

Lots of CEOs and business leaders talk about the importance of meditation and there have been countless studies that show meditation, or mindfulness, boosts productivity as well as mental calm by helping to develop the prefrontal cortex, the area of the brain which controls decision-making and awareness, and memory. Don't know how to start? Amisha Ghadiali advises taking it back to basics. 'Try closing your eyes and allowing a bit of mental stillness. The main thing you notice is you have so many thoughts, which is totally normal, but the less you get involved in your thoughts, the more space appears. If you don't play with them, they eventually go away.'

Digital detoxing

We're all increasingly reliant on our phones: it's where we do our banking, reply to emails on the go and read the news – never mind check social media. Horrifyingly, recent statistics show that a quarter of women in their thirties and a fifth of those in their forties check their phones 200 times a day. But our brains need a break, especially at night when the blue light from the screens can play havoc with the melatonin production in our brains, which signals that it's time to sleep.

I struggle to do this, but Amisha suggests banning technology from your bedroom and creating a work-free space, which will stop you mindlessly scrolling through social media if you wake up in the middle of the night.

Melissa Hemsley, chef and wellness influencer, says that she has recently done this: 'My new thing is that I switch my phone off at 6pm; if I need to post something to social media, I schedule that in advance. Then I do something meditative, even if that's just folding laundry, so that I unwind. I've found that it's had a huge effect on my anxiety levels. I'm also getting better at putting on an out of office when I go away. I used to be glued to my phone in case I missed a job, but now I have told myself, yes, I might miss something, but I will truly recharge. It's very freeing. You have to be OK with missing out on some things, because we're going to be working for a very long time; those opportunities will come around again.'

Spending time with yourself

When you've prioritised your work tasks, made time for your family and friends, plus factored in eating well and exercising, there's still one more date you need to make: a date with yourself.

Women are particularly bad at carving out this time for themselves, and I was definitely guilty of that when my children were very little. But it's essential if we don't want to end up on the floor. 'You need to find the time to replenish your cup,' agrees Amisha. 'The fuller your cup is, the more you have to give.' There's no need for an elaborate self-care routine (although you can if you want!). Personally, I try to read a book before bed, or watch a bit of television to totally switch my mind off from work.

The thing that goes hand-in-hand with this is actually investing in yourself. If you feel that you need to meditate, but meditation doesn't come naturally to you, seek out a teacher; if you struggle with exercise, then book a few sessions with a personal trainer, as I do, or go to a class with a friend; if it's a confidence coach you need, then seek that professional out. 'You need to have other people who are looking out for you with your best interests at heart to help you really shine,' Amisha says. It's really important to build up a support squad, even if that's paid professionals, so that all the pressure isn't solely on you.

CASE STUDY: ARIANNA HUFFINGTON, FOUNDER AND CEO OF THRIVE GLOBAL

Arianna Huffington is now the queen of balance, but it wasn't always the case. She was two years into founding the *Huffington Post* and working 18-hour days, as well as being a single mother to her two teenage daughters, when one morning she stood up to put on a sweater and collapsed.

When she woke up in a pool of blood, she was terrified, wondering what was wrong with her. Doctors told her that she had collapsed due to chronic exhaustion – and broken her cheekbone on the way down.

It was a huge wake-up call. She realised she needed to change her life dramatically. 'I had fallen complete prey to the delusion that in order to succeed as an entrepreneur and as a mother, I just had to sacrifice myself,' she says.

What's fascinating was her approach to solving the problem. She dedicated herself to sleep research and, as she got more into the details, she felt she had to share her findings. She launched a section on the *Huffington Post* dedicated to sleep, something she says she had trouble getting past her board: 'It's hard to go back to 2007 and see how disrespected sleep was. There was no way you would ever see an issue about sleep in the *Wall Street Journal* or the *Harvard Business Review* – which is now a regular place to find these conversations.'

She totally overhauled her own sleep routine, including her bedtime routine and bedroom environment. While she used to tap away on her phone up until the point at which she went to sleep, now she powers down 30 minutes before bedtime and leaves her devices outside the bedroom. She has a hot bath and puts on dedicated pyjamas, instead of wearing old gym clothes, as she used to, and reads a physical book. Finally, before turning off the light, she writes down three things she's grateful for, which she believes (and studies confirm) leads to better sleep and less night-time anxiety.

In 2014, she shared her message with the world with her book, *Thrive*, which was a global hit, and caught the attention of Jack Ma, co-founder and chair of Chinese tech giant Alibaba. He suggested that she could turn this into a business. He told her – fittingly, in his tai chi centre in China – that the scale of the stress problem he could see in China meant there must be a huge opportunity to change the landscape.

The idea kept circulating in her mind, and in 2016 she stepped down from the *Huffington Post* and launched the health and wellness media start-up Thrive, with one central aim of showing the importance of essential sleep and rejuvenation. She says now that she's grateful for her collapse because it showed her not only how damaging her lifestyle was, but how she could build a company dedicated to spreading that message. 'Burnout – and awareness about its dangers – is now a front-burner topic, both collectively and individually. It's a part of our everyday conversation and, collectively, it's finally coming to be regarded as the public health issue it is.'

CHAPTER RECAP: The Balancing Act

The concept of work – life balance is a bit of a myth and not realistic for modern work practices; we prefer to think of integrating life and work. But you do still need techniques to achieve harmony in your day and week and make sure that you're not investing too much energy into one section of your life.

Accepting you can't do it all: The first step is accepting you can't do everything. This means setting boundaries with yourself and others, and prioritising the most important jobs.

Children: We're having children older so we're further along in our careers. It's a good time to keep pushing yourself, if that's what you want to do, to advance your career. But you need a good support network at work and at home to help you.

Partners and friends: It's equally important to keep investing in relationships with partners and friends. These are key relationships you rely on to keep you sane and support you.

Wellbeing: Women tend to be bad at prioritising their own wellness, but it's important to do so in order to remain fighting fit. We need to take good care of our diet, exercise and sleep routines, even when it's tempting to neglect them in busy times.

Mental health: Our mental health is a huge priority, and we need strategies to help us cope with what can, at times, be overwhelming amounts of pressure and work.

Check in with yourself regularly to make sure you actually feel the best you can, not just OK. Lean on your support network if you need them.

Digital detox: We're surrounded by emails, texts, digital media and social media and it can be all-consuming. Our phones are designed to keep us addicted, and sometimes we need to set firm boundaries with ourselves over their use. We all need help powering down at times.

WORKSHEET: LEARNING THE BALANCING ACT

Everything we do requires energy and it's a precious resource. The more we can take responsibility for managing the energy we have, be it physical, mental or emotional, the more empowered and productive we become. The three exercises below should help you identify where you need to direct and conserve your energy in order to feel happier and more fulfilled.

1. Reflect on the following:

In your average working day, what drains you and what energises you?

_____

_____

_____

_____

How do you build more nourishing habits into your day/week so you have the foundation for a positive energy reservoir? (Consider when and what you eat, your sleeping habits, etc.)

_____

_____

_____

_____

2. Think about what activities give you positive emotions of enjoyment, challenge, adventure, opportunity. Now think about how you can allocate more time each day or week to these.

_____

_____

_____

_____

3. Identify one critical task you must achieve at work this week. (You can repeat this for as many tasks as you would like.) Think about what kind of mental input it requires (e.g., creativity, collaboration, reflection), what time of day is best for you to do it and what kind of environment you need to do it in (e.g. a quiet computer area, relaxed meeting area, a one-on-one space).

_____

_____

_____

_____

CHAPTER EIGHT

The Resilience Recipe

'The things you think are disasters in your life are not disasters really. Almost anything can be turned around. Out of every ditch, a path – if only you can see it'

Thomas Cromwell (Hilary Mantel, Bring Up the Bodies*)*

Debbie

Resilience is a business buzzword at the moment. Never before have we operated in such a fast-paced, frenetic world where we're permanently connected, never switching off. We've talked about how wellness is important to being able to maintain a semblance of sanity. Resilience, that ability to bounce back from bumps in the road, is the other key to avoiding burnout.

It's so important to have realistic expectations; business, just like life, is hard. There are always going to be setbacks; to be a success you need to know how to get up and fight another day. Why do we need to fight? Well, as US wrestler Ronda Rousey says (perhaps literally, although we agree metaphorically, too), 'You have to fight because you can't count on anyone else fighting for you.'

The reality is that plans rarely go smoothly. Every successful person I know has had failures and rejections – from the author J.K. Rowling's original Harry Potter manuscript that was rejected 12 times by publishers; to Naomie Harris, who says she's rejected on a weekly basis; to Sir James Dyson, who developed 5,126 prototypes that failed before he came up with the winning Dyson model. Kathleen Saxton, a psychotherapist by training as well as a founder and CEO, says, 'We've got to recognise that at some point you'll meet some level of resistance. That acceptance is important.'

I know a lot about resilience. When my marriage broke up, I suddenly found myself as a single mum with children aged under one and three. That certainly wasn't a life plan, and it felt like a very public failure. But there were very clear economic realities, and as an entrepreneur I felt that the only way out was to build my way out of it. My business, Love Home Swap, was born out of the ashes of that very dark time.

It wasn't an easy ride when we started. There was a point at the beginning of 2014 before closing an essential funding round when things looked pretty bleak. It felt like this might fail, too. And I remembered the quotation from the character of Thomas Cromwell, written by Hilary Mantel, that heads this chapter. I wrote it down and kept it on my desk because I find it so powerful; there are times when it still makes me feel emotional contemplating it. I've had whole weeks where I've read that again and again, every day.

Resilience can partly be about weathering the storm. You do need a thick 'rhino hide', both in top levels of business and on the way up. That's not to say that resilient people don't have the same feelings of disappointment, hurt or loss when something doesn't go to plan – we do. Instead, it's about learning to channel our emotions so that we can deal with what we need to in the moment, and then taking time after the event to reflect on what has happened and find that path out. Then you need to get back up. 'Most successful people can tell of times when they were knocked back,' Professor Lynda Gratton says. 'I've always tried to teach that to my own children when things have been tough for them, I say, OK, let's move on.'

That's not always easy, of course. The key is to tap into our sense of self and inner confidence by sticking to our vision and goals. Because when you remain fixed to what you believe is true and the right thing to do, you become less shakeable.

We've just talked about wellness strategies, and in the same vein you should consider shortcuts to resilience. Mine are rereading the quotation at the start of this chapter as well as tapping into my amazing sisterhood for support. Whatever your shortcut is, find it and use it. If you can bounce back and learn from it, you'll feel so much better equipped the next time a challenging situation arises, and your confidence will keep growing. You need to build up your resilience to last a career lifetime.

What can set us back

When a difficult situation arises, our brain has a lot to process. 'Our prefrontal cortex, the part where we rationalise things, starts to wonder what is *factually* going on,' explains Kathleen Saxton. 'But the limbic system, which deals with how we *feel*, kicks in a few milliseconds before our rational mind.' We all know how that feels. 'The warning signs could be a feeling of a flip of the stomach, that feeling that you can't think straight, or a sense of tightening in your throat that stops you speaking,' Kathleen says.

There are lots of things that can knock us back. There are the big things: death, illness, relationship breakdowns, job loss and business closures. Plenty of women in the public eye have weathered such storms and discovered their resilience. Both Bozoma 'Boz' Saint John, chief marketing officer at Endeavor, and Facebook's COO Sheryl Sandberg have spoken publicly about the deaths of their husbands. In a speech to Berkeley students, Sheryl said, 'I woke up on what I thought would be a totally normal day. And my world just changed for ever.' She spent the next two years pouring over academic studies to research the power of resilience. It's fair to say she's an expert in the topic. Meanwhile, Boz has talked about how her late husband Peter gave her the 'gift of urgency' and 'the grace' to get things done. 'Never settle for the things that you think are impossible to attain,' she told an audience at an African Leadership Initiative West Africa fundraiser dinner, 'and never take "no" for an answer. Do it right now'.

Those huge knocks are really, really hard, but fortunately they happen relatively infrequently. Actually it's often the day-to-day niggles that have bigger impacts on most us. As Lizzie Cho, director of Nova New Opportunities, says, its those things such as 'a really long commute, having a difficult relationship with your boss, not having a great team, or working towards a goal that is constantly moving away and feeling like the rug is being pulled from beneath you.'

Relationships in the office are also a huge part of this daily grind. You're thrown together with a group of people who have their own strengths, weaknesses, stresses and strains, and once hierarchies are added to the mix, it can be a heady cocktail of emotions and power plays. We probably spend more time with our colleagues than our partners or close friends, which, if a relationship turns sour, means it can be an uncomfortable situation within the political ecosystem.

Experiencing bullying in the workplace will often test resilience, while imposter syndrome can eat away at it. 'When things go wrong, women in particular tend to be knocked in self-confidence or competence,' Kathleen says. 'They think, "Am I good enough?" We often find with men that they gloss over the things they're not as good at. Women put focus of the blame on ourselves, which isn't healthy.' I agree that it is a fairly common female trait, and one we have to overcome.

The 10-step resilience plan

Just as we've built up confidence and wellness plans in previous chapters (and both are crucial to your resilience), so we want to address a resilience plan. While your upbringing definitely shapes you in terms of how mentally tough you are, the good news is that resilience is something that is built up over a lifetime and is something you can learn. When I started my first business aged 25, I was pretty tough, but there's no way I was as resilient as I am now. That's the benefit of living through those knocks and learning from them. So here is our practical recipe for resilience, drawn from our experience as well as our work sisterhood, who have collectively taken more knocks than Ronda.

1. Recognise that *everyone* suffers the knocks

The first rule of resilience club, according to Kathleen, is acknowledging to ourselves that we are experiencing a struggle, and validating those feelings, and then think, 'there will be a way through this'. The first thing to remember – which it can be hard to do in the moment – is that everyone suffers from embarrassing setbacks or even total failures. The actress Naomie Harris says the life of an actor – which she's been living since she was nine years old – is filled with daily rejections. 'I remember one particularly galling moment in my early career when I turned up to a premiere of a film I was in, walked the red carpet, gave interviews about my role, and then settled into my seat to watch the film with my friends and family … only to discover that I had not only been cut out of the movie, but replaced by a different actress and no one had told me!' It is something she's learned to find amusing. 'I laugh about that moment now, but I certainly wasn't laughing at the time.'

Or consider another woman in the public eye: Hillary Rodham Clinton. She has had some major career highs including being appointed Secretary of State in Barack Obama's cabinet and becoming the first female nominee for a major political party to run for President (read more about her career in chapter nine). But ultimately, she also had some *very* public setbacks that have included surviving an infidelity, losing the Democratic nomination to the young Senator from Illinois and subsequently losing out to Donald J. Trump to become the 45th President of the United States of America. As she said when speaking to Yale University's graduating class of 2018, 'Everyone gets knocked down, what matters is whether you get up and keep going. You will make mistakes in life, you will even fail, it happens to all of us, no matter how qualified and capable we are. Take it from me.' It's safe to say she knows a thing or two about resilience.

2. Hanging on to your inner confidence

A lot of resilience is about confidence, so to start with, remember why you're great and refer back to *Believe* to remind yourself of your strengths, your motivations and your confidence plan.

But the lesson that Naomie has learned, from reeling from the knocks of her profession, is 'don't have all your "confidence eggs" in your work basket'. Take time to build a sense of self outside of your job. 'I love my profession and the work I do, and my nominations and awards are a source of pride, but that isn't where I derive my self-worth,' Naomie says. 'To keep your confidence buoyant despite the inevitable knocks within any industry is incredibly important. My self-worth comes from things totally unrelated to work. My confidence comes from the way I strive to be the best possible version of myself I can be, my level of authenticity, and the kindness with which I treat both myself and other people.'

One tip Lizzie Cho recommends is finding a mantra that works for you. 'I was the arch cynic of mantras for most of my life,' she confesses, 'until I found one that I connected with: "I'm here, I want to be here, I deserve to be here." This really helped me. I said it until I really believed it and reflected on each part of it. You can find something that means something to you.' I've personally got a few mantras that I live by: sweat every day, eat healthily, connect with people who inspire you. They keep me going.

3. Set boundaries

If people are making unreasonable or unrealistic demands on you, be prepared to tell them how you feel and say 'no'. Women are often people pleasers, but trust us that a quick, efficient 'no' is better than coming back later and saying you can't do the job. 'The quicker you can do that, the quicker you can move on. You can say thank you, but no thank you,' Katy Koob, vice president of Refinery29 says.

Assertiveness is a tricky balance – and something that women are typically less good at. It involves being forthright about your wants and needs, while considering what needs to be done for your team and the business. But it's crucial to your resilience, and that of the business. If you don't think you can take on the extra work and do it justice, then it's vital to say so up front.

Setting boundaries in a business capacity can help, too. 'By thinking through what's important to you, set out where your boundaries are. Think in advance: what business opportunity would you say no to? What you would turn down helps you realise what you'd say yes to – and most importantly: WHY,' says Isabel Collins, founder of specialist consultancy Belonging Space.

Part two of this realism is knowing when to quit. We believe passionately in reaching high, dreaming big and working hard. But there are times when you just have to know when to stop. The problem with working on something you're passionate about is that it's really hard to turn it off. But it's important to recognise how to keep your resilience strong so that you can regroup and fight another day.

4. Develop a personal structure

There's a big misunderstanding around entrepreneurs and creatives that they are just unstructured, go-with-the-wind types of people. Actually, most people I know have a routine that they stick to every day. For instance, I start every day with a 6am boxing class. It gets me out of the door on even the toughest days and fired up for the day ahead, and helps me structure the rest of my day.

NneNne Iwuji-Eme, Britain's first black female diplomat (read more about her story in chapter nine), says structure is essential to helping her cope. She meditates for 10–15 minutes first thing in the morning, and again at night and hits the gym three times a week to relieve stress.

Lots of people have their own morning trick. There are reams of internet articles about it; we're seemingly obsessed with how successful people structure their mornings. One example I love, because it shows how small it can be, is the tip naval Admiral William McRaven revealed in his University of Texas at Austin commencement speech: 'If you make your bed every morning, you will have accomplished the first task of the day. It will give you a small sense of pride, and it will encourage you to do another task and another and another.' The point is that a small ritual starts to mean something; it lets you mentally tick off one easy task from the list and leads you on to the next thing on your to-do list. There will be some dark weeks – months, even – when it will feel like you've just got to knock the days off. If our business journey is a marathon, then can we just run for another mile (and then another mile), one foot after the other? A structure is part of your armour and it helps you battle through.

5. Dealing with conflict

We can face lots of mini aggressions on a daily basis, especially when things are stressful. Executive chair of Newsworks Tracy De Groose remembers a time when office politics was ruining her work life. 'As I got more senior in one organisation, I could feel the politics becoming more of a problem and I wasn't very good at dealing with one particular person. So I got a coach to help me with that. My coach said to me, "You're projecting what he's doing to you, back on to him, and no one likes to see their negative qualities reflected back. All he wants is to be listened to and valued." From that moment on all my conversations with this man completely changed. It was such simple advice, but sometimes you need people outside of the political ecosystem to spot them.' Dealing with the source of aggression, instead of letting it build, was crucial in this instance.

When Anna and I set out on this venture, we encountered rejection to start with, and then criticism. And this continues, as background noise, on most days. There are lots of people out there who don't like us or don't want to see us succeed – and so we say 'rhino hide' to each other daily to remind ourselves to shake it off. The higher you climb the harder the wind blows. The first time you are publicly criticised or you read something about yourself in print that's not nice is a key moment; rarely in life do we experience a public shaming, so it can sting at first. Now we usually find it funny – especially when it's wildly inaccurate (we have quite a dark sense of humour).

So, whether you've just pitched a new idea, or got feedback on a project or asked for a pay rise and received some negative news, you've got to somehow absorb it and then find a way to use the experience to grow. 'If you're having a "difficult conversation" then the more honest and relaxed you can be about it, the better,' Tracy advises. It helps to reframe the context; this often isn't really about you, it's a business decision.

We're going to cover this more in chapter ten, as well as how to effectively lean in to conflict when needed, and when to walk away.

6. Be gritty

Designer Anya Hindmarch recently said something that really struck a chord with me: 'Creativity is a real journey. First you love what you're doing, then you hate it, and then you hate yourself. That dip is a tough place to be. It's about holding your nerve.' That's true about business as much as designing a handbag. In the many nail-biting moments I've had with various businesses, I've just had to grit my teeth and wait it out. If you're the leader, you can't let too much of that worry seep through to your team, you have to try to absorb it.

The next thing you must do is recognise you already are resilient. It's unlikely that you've breezed through life without any setbacks already. It is really important to remember how you have already displayed inner grit in getting through these life experiences, and reflect on how you coped. 'That will inform you how you deal with things in the future,' Lizzie Cho says. Namely that you're still here and fighting.

7. Be realistic

You have to manage your expectations. Just as life isn't always upbeat and fulfilling every second of the day, you do have to realise that work isn't either. Sometimes things go right, sometimes they go wrong, you just have to accept that. Telling yourself that is a form of brain training – realigning our expectations and not setting ourselves up for a fall.

Sarah Wood agrees in the tough talk strategy. 'In 2008/9 business wasn't going well; [it felt like] every day a member of staff was being poached by Google or Facebook, we weren't making sales and it felt like a bad time. Then I would tell myself that in fact I wasn't down a coal mine, my kids didn't have to walk five miles to find a well for water, here I was in charge of my own company. I had to step back and look at the bigger picture and remind myself how lucky I was to be here, to work on this company, with people of my choosing. I am able to come in after dropping my kids off at school, whereas Maria the cleaner, has had to leave her kids in Romania to come here to work and send money home and only sees them four times a year. When you put your journey in the context of other people's, you soon remember how lucky you are.'

8. Reframing setbacks

The best and most innovative companies recognise failure as the by-product of the bravery needed to take risks and experiment. Leading psychologist Dr Martin Seligman, says the way that we explain setbacks to ourselves has a big impact on our resilience, so instead of thinking, 'Why does this always happen to me?', accept that failure happens and reframe it as a problem-solving opportunity.

Cassandra Stavrou, co-founder of the snack company Propercorn, had huge success at the start of her business journey, when she was stocked in the staff canteen at Google HQ UK. But she says she's made lots of mistakes, too. 'When we launched we didn't understand shelf life: we thought a six-month shelf life meant we had six months to shift the product. But retailers demand at least four months' shelf life at the point at which it goes into their depot. So really, we only had two months to sell it and get it stocked; we hadn't forecast for that. It could have bankrupted our business in terms of cash flow, but it put pressure on us to follow every lead, cold call clients, and leave no stone unturned in our sales effort. It ended up catapulting our sales.'

Even if you can't turn the setback into a success story like Cassandra, I think there's something comforting about the idea that every little knock you endure makes you stronger. Eleanor Roosevelt said, 'You gain strength, courage, and confidence by every experience in which you really stop to look fear in the face. You're able to say to yourself, "I've lived through this horror, I can take the next thing that comes along."' It's really true. Once you're through this horror, you will look back and be proud about how you weathered the storm.

9. Be kind to yourself

'Being your kind inner voice is essential,' Sarah Wood adds. 'I make sure I talk to myself in a positive way.' It's great advice – lots of people are their own harshest critic, when in fact we've found there are plenty of other people who will be that for you!

Learning not to take failure personally is hard. But it's essential. I've had to learn it – it's not something I naturally had as a skill, no one does. But people who have a strong resilience don't automatically blame themselves when something doesn't go according to plan; they might be more circumspect and look at potential other causes. So instead of thinking, 'I messed that project up because I can't do my job,' they would look to a lack of support. I've known that some ideas I've had have just been terrible timing for the market, and that's why they've failed to take off, rather than necessarily being bad ideas.

It's our job to be our own personal champions. Imagine what you would say to your best friend if she were in your position and channel that. This includes if you've done a job well, or completed a goal, rewarding yourself. It doesn't have to be much: a little 'well done me', or a walk around the park will do, but you do need to recognise and take mental note when something has gone well. Think of it as your personal appraisal, from yourself, to yourself.

10. Lean on your sisterhood

If you don't have the resilience you need – and none of us do *all* the time – that's when you need to find someone who can be there for you when you dip. When Anna and I are together, we measure each other's resilience levels, and step in as needed.

Networks both inside and outside your workplace can really help bolster your resilience. 'Having a network is critical to staying strong,' Sarah Wood advises. 'There's nothing like sitting down with someone else over a cup of tea, chatting through and sharing your problems, and coming up with solutions together. In the early days, one of the most helpful things was talking with other COOs in the tech world who were facing similar issues with product and scaling. It was so cathartic to be able to realise that you're not alone and to look at how each other was fixing problems. It was transformative for me in building up my resilience.' We've found the same: by looking after each other, we're stronger together.

CASE STUDY: WHITNEY WOLFE HERD, FOUNDER AND CEO OF BUMBLE

We all know Whitney Wolfe Herd as the inspirational CEO who has transformed the online dating world for women with her app, Bumble. But the idea actually came from a very dark moment in her personal life, when she had to dig deep into her resilience and fight her way back out on top.

In 2014 she had just left Tinder, the company she had co-founded and helped build up to the global success it is now. But she left in a storm, alleging in a lawsuit that was settled out of court that she had been sexually harassed. She left a job she had loved, a company she helped build and a town that she had called home for two years. 'I lost that sense of belief in myself,' she says.

Coupled with that, she was plagued by online abuse. The ordeal sent her into a depression. 'I started to believe what people had been saying about me online and it really had a detrimental effect on my value and worth. It's difficult to brush things off when people are saying such nasty things about you. I wish I had the resilience I have now, then.' But it also sparked her creativity. Whitney had been an entrepreneur since she was 19 and founded her own company selling tote bags to raise funds for areas affected by the BP oil spill in the Gulf of Mexico. Now she decided to use her experience to change the online world for women. She came up with a new idea for a female-only social network that valued kindness and good online behaviour – instead of the lewd and rude world that the internet could be. She called her network Merci.

Meanwhile, Andrey Andreev, founder and CEO of Badoo, the largest dating platform in the world, got in touch and asked her to come to London for a meeting. He wanted her to work for him in-house as chief marketing officer. In a negotiating masterstroke, she turned the conversation around, refusing his job offer, but instead telling him about her new idea. He loved it, but thought it would be brilliant for the dating world. He offered her funding and access to his technical team.

She did it, launching Bumble, the dating app where women make the first move. It prides itself in valuing and encouraging principles including integrity, kindness, equality, confidence and respect both online and offline. 'At Bumble, we keep everything grounded in our values: kindness, equality, accountability and empowering women across the globe,' she says.

Since then, 40 million people have signed up, with over 3 billion messages sent. More than 60,000 people download it every day and those numbers are rising. Whitney, as its CEO, has been listed in Forbes 30 under 30, and the app and its remit is expanding. Along with its business networking arm, Bumble Bizz, the company has recently launched an investment fund specifically for women founders.

Whitney explains, 'Even though that situation ultimately fuelled my innate desire to create something which stopped this happening to other people, I had to go through a pretty tough road to get there. But the advice I would give my younger self is to believe in myself no matter what. I've learned that we take chances, we make mistakes and we learn lessons. I've learned that if you can identify a problem and find a way that technology can enable the solution – you're onto a winning formula.'

CHAPTER RECAP: Resilience

Those who develop a level of resilience are not only able to weather the storm, but also to bounce back and learn from the experience.

Remember it happens to us all: The first step is to recognise that everyone suffers from knocks and setbacks – that's just life. Tap into your strong sense of self and believe in your own power.

Set your boundaries: Decide where your own line in the sand is and be prepared to say 'no' and explain why if people are making unreasonable or unrealistic demands on you. It will help keep your life balanced and prevent you from burnout.

Create your own timetable: A structure to your day can form part of your armour and help you battle through. Develop little routines, such as an early morning exercise habit, to help you take on the day.

Deal with conflict: We can face lots of instances of conflict on a daily basis. You have to develop a rhino hide and learn how to deal with the situations that arise.

Be gritty: In some situations you just have to grit your teeth and wait it out, counting off each day at a time.

Reframe setbacks: Some failures or bumps in the road can be turned around quickly and made into success stories. Others can't, but they are still learning experiences that the best companies actually relish.

Be kind to yourself: Turn off that inner critic and instead talk to yourself the way you would a friend. It's our job to be our own personal champions.

Lean on your sisterhood: There's no need to shoulder all of life's burdens alone; it is actually a sign of strength to lean on allies in times of need. Build up these networks and support others, so that in times of need you have your sisterhood to hand.

WORKSHEET: BUILDING RESILIENCE

A key building block to establishing resilience is reframing setbacks accurately. For this we need to be aware of, and banish, negative thoughts.

Write down the two–three times you recently have thought the following:

- 'Why does this always/only happen to me?'
- 'I'm such a failure'
- 'I'm a bad ...'
- 'I should be more ...' or 'I should be less ...'
- 'Everything is wrong'

_____

_____

_____

_____

Once you have identified your negative thoughts, work with someone to reflect on what might be a more accurate and useful thought, one that, while still honest, will allow you to move forward. How can you reframe those thoughts?

_____

_____

_____

_____

The next step in building resilience is learning from the mistakes you make. Take time to reflect on mistakes or failures you may have made over the last month or so. Think about lessons you can pull from them. Every mistake has the power to teach you something important. Start by noting one or two such instances below.

_____

_____

_____

_____

BECOME.

You have worked through **Believe** and **Build** and so you should have a strong sense of what you want to achieve and how to start work on the practical steps to make that happen. This section is the icing on the cake. It really helps to believe it if you can actually see it, so we've profiled 15 inspirational women who have worked their way to the top – and crucially how they got there. Navigating the path to the top involves negotiation skills: we all use them every day, and there's a definite art. Then you need to work on your hustle. It's a word associated with the entrepreneurial world, but it applies just as much to those working in business, too. It's about spotting opportunities, going for them and working damn hard to turn them into success stories. Underpinning this whole book, as you'll have picked up, is that the power of your sisterhood can help with all these steps. We know it, and the women interviewed in this book know it: sisterhood works. Get out there and build up yours to help you become who you want to be.

CHAPTER NINE

A Pioneer

'Glass ceilings have been broken, but more have to be broken'

Madeleine Albright

Anna

My story of breaking through the glass ceiling is one of becoming the first CEO of Hearst magazines UK, a company that has a history of more than 100 years, that counted a third of British women among its audience but had never had a female CEO in the UK, and where at board level men were largely in charge.

When I was offered the big job, obviously I was thrilled, but I also had to think long and hard: could I deal with this structure? At the top, where ultimately the strategy for the business is signed off, I would be working with predominantly older men. Would I be able to get my voice heard and deliver on the role as I was expected to in a way that felt authentic to me? I knew there would be added pressure being the first woman CEO because all eyes would be on me, as they are on the other sprinkling of women who make up just 7 per cent of the CEOs of FTSE 100 companies and 5 per cent of Fortune 500 companies. Being the first female comes with a weight of responsibility: to paraphrase Madeleine Albright, there's no room for a mediocre female CEO.

Of course, I accepted the job, and the number of emails and letters I received from women in the company was unbelievable. Not because they wanted me in particular to be the boss, but because of what it meant. They wrote things like, 'Finally I can see there's a path; working here makes sense.' You have to realise that sometimes things like this are bigger than just you. As Newsworks's Tracy De Groose says, 'Remember, as a woman working towards a more senior position you are creating opportunities for future women to succeed. Whether you like it or not, you are a flag-bearer for the next generation, leading by example.'

So, the million-dollar question: how do you do it? There's not a single route, as you will know, but there are some building blocks you need in place. You've got to go through the stages that we've detailed in the chapters up to here: you need to know yourself inside out, develop rock-solid confidence (or at least a rock-solid game face), have your personal brand worked out and make sure you know your numbers. And then grab those opportunities with both hands. We all need to channel Alexandria Ocasio-Cortez, who at the start of 2018 was a cocktail waitress, then 10 months later, aged 29, made history by becoming the youngest woman elected to the US Congress with an astonishing 78 per cent of the vote.

My breakthrough came because I cared a lot about the brands, the consumers, the people I worked with and for, and the chance to start to take the company down a new path. I was obviously capable, but I'd made myself indispensable, and that was key. You know that as a middle manager you have to manage down. But managing up is just as crucial. Broadly speaking, it's about making your boss's job easier. It's not often said, but if you want to move up and shatter the glass ceiling, then you have to help your boss move up, sideways or out of the way.

You can't do this on your own, and this is where your networks come in. You need someone to champion you. In my case, my most pivotal career breaks were while I was working for two very different men. They couldn't have been more different to each other and I certainly had to adapt my approach with both of them.

My first jump into executive management came while I was working for a tough, blunt, very driven chairman. A lot of colleagues found him difficult to deal with, but I found we had common ground; he was a northerner, like me, and a father to four girls, while I was one of four sisters. His very dark sense of humour even reminded me of my dad's.

During my tenure at the company, I acquired a reputation as a fixer as I often put my hand up for tricky roles or projects that no one else wanted to do. This meant I was offered lots of different roles within the company, which ultimately propelled me up the career ladder to become chief operating officer of Hearst in the UK when Hachette and Natmag merged.

My first boss at Hearst was French and came from a very different work culture to the way we work in the UK. He was accustomed to hierarchical work environments and a different style of leadership, and I could see where I could help him and be a bridge between the two systems. It worked, we delivered well in a challenging environment, and when he decided to move on to a bigger role, he championed me as his 'heir apparent' ready to take over as CEO.

Both of these bosses were essentially 'sponsors' of mine – people who took an active role in my career path. However, you also need a wider support network of people, both inside and outside the organisation. This doesn't happen by accident and you have to have built up strong working relationships throughout your career with people who are willing to champion you. For those top jobs, people tend to ask around. The Hearst board spoke to all our key suppliers, stakeholders and buyers as well as to my colleagues and team to ask about me and my reputation before they offered me the role of CEO. Luckily, I'd built up good networks.

We still don't have enough women at the top of all areas in business and society, but what we are getting better at is sharing our stories. Debbie and I count some pretty exceptional women among our friends and business contacts who are firsts in their field and their stories are all inspirational. A lot of the confidence to progress is the ability to imagine yourself doing the job. This can be summarised by the well-known saying, 'you've got to see it to be it'. So, in that vein, here are 15 influential women, some of whom we know, the rest we admire from afar, who have all risen to the top of their respective industries in very different ways. It is not, of course, an exhaustive list, but it gives us all inspiration and background on how these extraordinary women all shattered the glass ceiling.

What you'll learn in this chapter:

- How to use the power of networks to get to the top
- Why authenticity is key to your success

- Why you need confidence
- The importance of resilience
- How risk-taking pays off

Fifteen inspirational stories from women at the top

We all take different routes to the top, but the women below display lots of the skills and mindsets that we've detailed in the book so far, from employing the calculated risk-taking of an entrepreneur to building a rock-solid confidence and belief in yourself, to maintaining your authenticity, even when others question you. Don't take this list as definitive – use it as a springboard to read more about the countless stories of female firsts around the world, and talk to trail-blazing women in your own network about their journeys. By sharing stories, we can make change happen.

Madeleine Albright, diplomat. First female Secretary of State in US history

Madeleine is a very special female first to us. It was her words, 'There is a special place in hell for women who don't help other women', that inspired our business. Fiercely bright, she studied for a Master's degree at Columbia University (she would later earn another Master's and PhD), and interned on a newspaper where she met Joseph Albright. They married soon after she graduated in 1959 and had three daughters. She later said, 'As much as I loved being a mother, I could not figure out why I had gone to college just to figure out how to get them in and out of the apartment or give them baths.'

Madeleine began to get involved in the Washington political scene, working as a political fundraiser and later serving as the chief legislative assistant in President Jimmy Carter's government. Ever the networker, her home became a hub for influential Democratic politicians and policy-makers.

Albright's political star began to rise when President Bill Clinton named her ambassador to the United Nations in 1993, before appointing her Secretary of State, making her the first woman to hold that office in the United States. Among her many achievements is being the first ever US Secretary of State to visit North Korea (albeit in peace talks that ultimately failed), as well as paving the way for two further female Secretaries of State: Condoleezza Rice and Hillary Rodham Clinton. She famously supported Hillary during her presidential bids in 2008 and 2016. During the later campaign, Madeleine wore a brooch made of shattered glass. She tweeted: 'After tonight, this pin will be the only piece of glass ceiling left at #DNCinPHL!'. Now that is power dressing.

Oprah Winfrey, entrepreneur and broadcaster. First woman to own and produce her own talk show and first black female entrepreneur listed on Bloomberg billionaires' list

Oprah started her career as a TV news anchor, but found that the role of just presenting the facts – and not being able to empathise with her interviewees – 'never felt authentic to me. I always felt like I had a pretend voice when I went on the air.' She was famously sacked from the role and moved to a talk show. Her natural warmth and empathy were rewarded when a Chicago TV station invited her to host her own morning show, leading on to the job that we know her best for, *The Oprah Winfrey Show*. It was a nationally syndicated programme and went out on 120 channels across the US with an audience of 10 million people. Which meant big money: the show grossed $125 million by the end of its first year, from which Oprah received a reported $30 million. 'I remember going to my bosses once we were syndicated,' she has said. 'I was making a lot of money, and my producers were still getting the same salary.' In an astonishing response, her boss replied, 'They're only girls. They're a bunch of girls. What do they need more money for?' Oprah refused to work until they were paid more, paying the women in the interim herself. The power of sisterhood in action.

Jody Gerson, chairman and CEO of Universal Music Publishing Group. First woman to run a major music publishing company

After starting in the music industry in the photocopier room, Jody scored an early hit when at the music company EMI: she signed a 15-year-old Alicia Keys. She repeated her success by discovering the then unknown Stefani Germanotta, later known to the world as Lady Gaga. Seven years on, she'd risen up the ranks to the role of co-president and felt there was nowhere left to go. She was offered the chief executive role at a rival company (UMPG). 'I didn't "have a gut" about it, but what I did have a gut about was: all these men were getting big gigs and I was just as good as them, so why wasn't I getting them?'

Her new role meant she was the first female to run a major music publishing company. Her roster of artists includes megastars like Adele and Ariana Grande, and under her leadership the company has seen a 30 per cent jump in revenues, while Jody has been awarded music industry press Billboard's 'visionary' accolade. But, she says, 'It's not enough that there's only one [female] chairman of a global music company. There should be more than one. But we're not going to get there unless we support each other and put each other in that position.'

Alexandria Ocasio-Cortez, politician. The youngest woman to serve in Congress in the history of the United States of America

When she took office in January 2019, Alexandria was officially the youngest woman to serve in Congress, and her rise to power has been meteoric. Only ten months before she won the election, as the newspapers were delighted to point out, she was working as a waitress in the Bronx in New York, where she was brought up. Of course, it runs deeper than the headlines like to make out. Alexandria has always had a strong political conscience, and had been working away behind the scenes.

Working as an educator at the non-profit National Hispanic Institute and used her passion for education and social justice to set up the publishing firm Brook Avenue Press, specialising in children's literature. She also campaigned for

Bernie Sanders in the 2016 election. But she might also be the only congresswoman to have an asteroid named after her: while she was at high school, she won second prize in the Intel International Science and Engineering Fair. As part of her prize, the International Astronomical Union named a small asteroid after her: 23238 Ocasio-Cortez. They could obviously tell she was destined for the stars.

Stacey Cunningham, trader. First woman to become president of the New York Stock Exchange

Stacey started at the New York Stock Exchange as an 18-year-old intern, while studying industrial engineering at Lehigh University. The internship led to a job, and she became one of only a couple of dozen women working among more than a thousand men. 'There were about 1,300 men at the Exchange when I became a member, and roughly 30 women,' she said. 'I definitely stood out as a woman on the trading floor, but I never felt singled out … I played my own game. I didn't try to be one of them. If you're trying too hard to be the way somebody else is, you're probably not going to be as successful.'

Her path into the organisation was originally made by a pioneering woman, Muriel Siebert, who became the first female member in the institution's then 175-year-history in 1967. She had to get sponsored by male members and the first nine men turned her down. According to Stacey, when Muriel did finally become a member, there was no ladies' toilet on the 7th floor, so a tiny phone booth was converted into one. 'When I started my career on the trading floor back in the mid-nineties, there was still this tiny little phone booth bathroom,' Stacey has said. A tiny monument to the women who made the first breakthrough.

NneNne Iwuji-Eme, ambassador. First black female UK career diplomat appointed high commissioner

When NneNne Iwuji-Eme was growing up, her parents, who worked for the UN, often invited contacts back to their home to discuss business. It meant that from a young age she was surrounded by people shaping policy. NneNne was born in Cornwall, but lived in various countries as a child and learned five languages, a skill that no doubt helped her during the 16 years she has worked for the Foreign Office.

Her appointment in 2018 as the first black female high commissioner really made waves. She said at the time in an official statement: 'I hope my appointment will inspire young talent, regardless of race or background, to pursue their ambitions in the Foreign Office.' In tribute to the way she was raised, she takes her nine-year-old son (who is already trilingual) on diplomatic missions. 'He's going to experience things you can't learn in a textbook. I want him to lap it all up.'

Dame Inga Beale, businesswoman. First female CEO of Lloyd's of London

Inga started her career in insurance after an internship at the British company, Prudential. She impressed them so much, they offered the accounting and economics Oxford graduate a job and she trained as an underwriter.

The culture at the firm in the eighties was, she has said, very sexist. Posters of women in bikinis would be left up around the office, and after she complained, she found her colleagues had wrapped them around her work station. At the time she was in a relationship with a woman, but didn't dare reveal it. 'I gave a clear instruction to my partner not to phone me in the office because I was so worried about my colleagues suspecting that I was having a relationship with a woman.' The strain of hiding her personal life was considerable – 'It eats away at you' – and, after a year off, she first went back to Prudential before becoming an underwriter in General Electric's insurance division, where she started to take on leadership positions.

She headed Swiss reinsurer Converium and joined the Zurich Insurance Group as a member of their group management board, where, she says, she publicly came out as bisexual: 'I decided to come out during the interview process so that I wasn't going into it with any secrets. I just brought it up with the group CEO and he was fine ... When I came out people were nervous talking about LGBT issues, although it has moved on' – largely thanks to the bravery and honesty of people including Inga.

Her career continued its trajectory, and in December 2013 she was announced as the new CEO of Lloyd's of London, becoming the first female CEO in the insurance market's 328-year history. Her appointment came 40 years after Liliana Archibald was the first woman to become a broker at the company. After her first day Liliana is said to have commented that 'the roof was still on'. Inga blew it off.

Emma Walmsley, CEO GlaxoSmithKline. First woman to run a major pharmaceutical company

Emma's appointment to the top of the pharmaceutical company GlaxoSmithKline (GSK) can be traced back to a networking lunch. She had been working for L'Oréal for 17 years, where she held a variety of general management and marketing roles, when she met the then CEO of GSK, Sir Andrew Witty. He persuaded her to move to GSK, something she later wrote that she felt was 'too risky' and 'disloyal' to her former employer. In a moment familiar to many women, she recalled asking herself if she was really qualified for the role. 'I spent a week persuading myself I would be insane to do it,' she recalled. When Sir Andrew left the company six years later, she was asked to fill his shoes, the first woman to do so. It created such waves that she was awarded number one on Fortune's International Power 50 list. Proof that networking works.

Baroness Brenda Hale, British judge. First woman president of the Supreme Court of the United Kingdom

Baroness Brenda Hale is a true pioneer. In 2017, at the age of 72, she smashed the ultimate barrier in her field, by becoming the first president of the Supreme Court, the UK's top appeals court.

But she had been testing boundaries her whole career. When she studied law at the University of Cambridge in the 1960s, she was one of six women out of a class of over 100. After graduating top of the class, she spent much of her early career in teaching, rising to become a professor of law at the University of Manchester, as well as working for the Law Commission, the official law reform body. In 2003, Dame Brenda Hale, as she was then, was one of three women judges in the Court of Appeal when she was confirmed as the UK's first woman law lord. The following year she joined the House of Lords as a Lord of Appeal in Ordinary, the only woman to have been appointed to this position.

At the time she was denounced by a national UK newspaper for being a 'hardline feminist'. She has consistently campaigned for more diversity among judges, noting in a lecture, 'There are plenty of able lawyers around from whom to pick a judiciary which would be more reflective of the general population – more women, more religious and ethnic minorities, more varied social and educational backgrounds, more varied professional backgrounds.' In democracy, and in business, diversity matters.

Dame Marjorie Scardino, business executive. First woman to head a FTSE 100 company and first woman on Twitter's board of directors

You might expect a bit of risk-taking from a former rodeo rider, and Marjorie Scardino has done just that. She started her career as a lawyer, rising up to managing partner of a law firm in Georgia, USA, when she and her husband launched a weekly newspaper. It was a huge success editorially, winning a Pulitzer Prize, but failed financially; she and her husband were forced to sell it for a dollar. The experience, she says, shaped her attitude to business: 'I learned then that you can fail and you don't die.' It also ignited a love of the media business.

Leaving law behind, she worked in the New York offices of *The Economist*, rising to president of the Economist Newspaper Group, Inc., where she more than doubled the magazine's North American circulation. She was then its chief executive officer for three years before being asked in 1997 to step up to be CEO of the British media firm Pearson PLC, making her the first woman to head a FTSE 100 company. She helped steer the company through investments in digital initiatives, navigate two recessions, a dotcom meltdown and the structural decline of print media.

She left in 2012 on a high: Pearson's share price had climbed almost 90 per cent under her 16-year leadership and *Forbes* magazine listed her as the 17th most powerful woman in the world. The *Telegraph* wrote at the time that her legacy was that 'she [had] raised the bar for female ambition and made the rest of the largely white and male corporate community take a harder look at their own boards.'

Liv Garfield, CEO Severn Trent. The FTSE 100's youngest female chief executive

Liv Garfield displayed obvious ambition from the start of her career, but says her 'big break was probably joining BT's executive committee' when she was 31. After three years of being chief executive of a division within BT, she was appointed as chief executive of Severn Trent, one of the largest regional water supply and sewerage businesses in the UK.

It was a turbulent time to join the company – months earlier it had seen off a £22-a-share hostile approach. But since she joined, the company's share price has risen and profits increased. She credits her success with her strong resilience: 'My philosophy is to begin every day afresh ... I've never looked back and said that I should have done something differently, but some days are harder than others.'

Hillary Rodham Clinton, politician. First female presidential candidate nominated by a major party

Hillary Rodham Clinton wasn't the first woman to stand for President. That accolade goes to Victoria Woodhull, who in 1872 became the first female presidential candidate, nearly 50 years before women could even vote. But in the 2016 presidential election, Hillary did become the first presidential candidate nominated by a major party.

Hillary has a history of breaking ground. A trained lawyer, she was appointed the first female chair of the Legal Services Corporation in 1978, before becoming the first female partner at her law firm a year later. But her career took a backseat while her husband Bill's political ambitions took centre stage. As First Lady of the United States she became the first working mother in the White House and had to field attacks on her character. She had more difficulties to come when her marriage was hit by the scandal involving her husband and Monica Lewinsky. She became an emblem of resilience and the couple's marriage endured.

After Bill's presidency ended, she decided to go into politics herself. In 2000, she was elected the first female Senator from New York and was re-elected in 2006. Two years later she set her sights on the highest office in American politics, but lost the Democratic party's official nomination to Barack Obama, who would later appoint her Secretary of State from 2009 to 2013. In 2016, she decided to run again for President, this time securing the official Democratic Party nomination. At points it looked certain that she would win the race and become the first female president of the United States of America. But she fell at the final hurdle.

It was a hard defeat to bear, but Hillary said afterwards that the mere fact that a woman ran for President had left its mark: 'Although we were not able to shatter that highest and hardest glass ceiling this time, thanks to you it has 18 million cracks in it, and the light is shining through like never before, filling us all with the hope and the sure knowledge that the path will be a little easier next time.'

Kiran Mazumdar-Shaw, entrepreneur. First woman in the world to win the Othmer Gold Medal for services to science through entrepreneurship

In 1978, aged just 25, Kiran Mazumdar-Shaw founded Biocon, an industrial-enzymes company and India's largest biopharmaceutical firm. The company was so successful that she became the first woman in the world to win the Othmer Gold Medal for services to science through entrepreneurship in 2014 and also India's first (and only!) self-made female billionaire, according to Forbes. What motivated her? 'One of my objectives when I started Biocon was to make sure that

I create a company for women scientists to pursue a vocation,' she has said. A shining example of sisterhood.

Sara Blakely, entrepreneur. Youngest self-made female billionaire in history

The entrepreneur Sara Blakely started her career selling fax machines door to door before she came up with the idea for Spanx. Once she had developed the product and got it into department stores, she knew that she needed sales to keep her stockists interested. So, she used her network and asked everyone she knew to purchase Spanx – reimbursing them later. She kept her day job while working on her side hustle, but when Oprah said the garments were one of her 'favourite things' in 2000, Sara was able to work on it full-time, eventually building up the sales and the company to the billion-dollar business it is today, with every celebrity rushing to endorse the power of her pants. When Forbes listed her as a billionaire in 2012 at the age of 41, she was the world's youngest self-made billionaire.

Dhivya Suryadevara, businesswoman. First CFO at General Motors

After Dhivya Suryadevara's father died when she was a child, her mother was left to raise three children on her own in Chennai, India. Determined her children would have the best in life, she instilled ambition in them. After a degree and Master's in India, Dhivya moved to America to study for an MBA at Harvard Business School. She has spoken about how the move to a new country, away from her support network was tough, but still, she thrived. The MBA led to an internship at the World Bank in 2002 before she joined UBS as an investment banker and, shortly after, moved to General Motors, where she has worked for 14 years.

She has doggedly worked her way up, heading up divisions of the company before landing the job of CFO – the first woman in the car maker's 110-year-history – last year. Her appointment makes General Motors one of only two Fortune 500 companies to have both a female CEO (Mary Barra has been the chairman and CEO of General Motors since 2014) and CFO. Proving that once the glass ceiling gets its initial cracks, change can follow quickly.

CHAPTER RECAP: A Pioneer

These stories are all inspiring and show very different routes to the top, but there are some common traits.

Power of networks: Madeleine Albright turned her Washington home into a salon for political movers and shakers, and it evidently helped her career. Emma Walmsley's top job can be traced back to a networking lunch. Networking works.

Authenticity: Oprah Winfrey found that straight news presenting didn't feel authentic to her, so she moved to chat show hosting, and from there her career took off. Inga Beale found that when she was authentic and honest about her sexuality, she was able to focus on the work ahead, rather than the effort of concealing her personal life, and in doing so will have inspired countless others to be authentic to themselves.

Graft and persistence: All of the women have put in the hard graft, working their way up their professions, but Brenda Hale shows that the hard route to the top can take a whole lifetime of work. Don't give up.

Confidence: Despite being one of only a handful of women on the trading floor, Stacey Cunningham says she never assumed she shouldn't be there. Emma Walmsley had to build up her confidence to compete at the top. Both show that you need it to succeed.

Resilience: Hillary Rodham Clinton is the ultimate emblem of resilience. She has suffered setbacks in both her personal and professional life, but she has returned to fight another day. Similarly, Oprah Winfrey was sacked from an early job, but it led on to greater things. While Sara Blakely struggled to get her product off the ground, it's now a billion-dollar business. The knocks are not always the end.

Leadership: Liv Garfield and Dhivya Suryadevara are a great example of how to position your career from a young age into leadership roles by spotting opportunities and putting your hand up for everything.

Risk-taking: Marjorie Scardino has all the risk-taking appetite of an entrepreneur. It hasn't always paid off – her venture into newspaper publishing was a financial failure. But the venture propelled her career in another direction and heightened her appetite for taking chances.

Sisterhood works: Another key quality all these women display is a keenness to help other women out behind them. Keep this in mind as you, too, rise up the ranks.

WORKSHEET: ADOPTING PIONEERING QUALITIES

Now you're inspired, it's time to turn that feeling into action. Try thinking about three qualities you admire most in the mini biographies you've just read and what specific action you can take to boost your career. Perhaps you feel you could improve your network, like Madeleine Albright, and you need to email a contact to suggest a drink, with a specific topic or idea to discuss. Or perhaps you could be bolder and take a risk like Marjorie Scardino – what project or initiative could you sign up for next? Write them below because, as we often say, what gets written down, gets done.

Quality 1 _____

What I need to do next:

_____

_____

Quality 2 _____

What I need to do next:

_____

_____

Quality 3 _____

What I need to do next:

_____

_____

CHAPTER TEN

The Art of Negotiation

'The most common way people give up their power is
by thinking they don't have any'

Alice Walker

Debbie

What's the first thing you think about when you hear the word negotiation? Money. Indeed, money is at the heart of the majority of negotiations, with the most common negotiations being about securing a pay rise. Here's how not to do it: if someone tries to persuade me that they need a pay rise because they are about to buy a house, or they think colleague X is being paid more than them or that they've been here for three years and it's time … well, it's just not going to wash. Those things might be true, and I've heard them all and plenty of variations on those themes, but in terms of negotiating for a pay rise, in a business sense they are meaningless. There is a much better way to frame the subject of a pay rise and we will teach the secrets of how to do it effectively and with confidence in this chapter.

We all negotiate every day, on subjects big and small. The key to a successful negotiation boils down to two key factors:

preparation and practice. Women in particular should definitely ask for pay rises more often, especially in light of the gender pay gap that exists in the UK and the USA, but we have to be better at doing it. Linda Babcock, a professor of economics at Carnegie Mellon University and the author of *Women Don't Ask*, has found that in studies of business school students, men initiate salary negotiations four times as often as women do.

'It's partly on us to ask for equality in pay, and become better negotiators on behalf of ourselves,' Jody Gerson, chairman and CEO of Universal Music Publishing Group, has said. She's right – Professor Babcock found that when women do negotiate, they ask for 30 per cent less than men do. This obviously means that men will get paid more. Helena Morrissey has said, 'I've even interviewed women who have pitched their salary expectations too low for the role and when I've queried it, hinting as much, they come back with an even lower figure.'

There is a much better way to frame the subject of a pay rise and in this chapter we will teach you how to do it effectively and with confidence.

Negotiations are not just about the big asks, they are about the small, daily ones, too. They are in the way that we frame a meeting or a conference call. Oprah starts every meeting the same way. She says: 'What is our intention for this meeting? What's important? What matters?' It's a great way of focusing the whole team on getting the best out of the negotiation.

I have to negotiate every single day. I've done all sorts of deals – bought and sold businesses, hired people, raised tens of millions of dollars in capital. I see negotiation as another language: the language of deals. You've got to have a map where you've figured out what you want, what the other party wants, where you're prepared to compromise and concede ground, and where your red line is. It's like a battle plan. That's a learned skill – when I was younger, I didn't realise this and didn't always go into a negotiation knowing where I wanted to end up. I do now.

Traditionally, negotiations are seen as situations where someone wins and someone loses – but that's a really macho way of approaching a negotiation. I think a successful negotiation is one where each party feels they've won. That's not to say I don't drive a hard bargain – I do – but I think it's important that everyone's happy with the deal, especially when you need to establish an ongoing working relationship.

If Anna and I are going into an investment meeting, we not only learn all our facts and figures, but we role-play and ask each other the killer questions. You need to be ready with all the answers, particularly if you're a woman in negotiations dominated by men. They often love to try to catch you out, and can smell weakness a mile off. Amanda Staveley, CEO of PCP Capital Partners, has said that 'Men tend to be more aggressive when there are a lot of them and they all know each other well, though being the only woman can actually be advantageous – it's never a bad thing to be underestimated.' It's so true. Underestimate us at your peril.

Negotiations quite often have moments where they are uncomfortable, as you carve out a deal, or even as you broach the topic. But don't be afraid of upsetting the balance or spending time in the discomfort zone – just do your preparation and go for it. If you lean in to some of those challenging conversations with positive intent and curiosity, you'll find they get easier every time. Practice really does make perfect.

What you'll learn in this chapter:

- How to get a pay rise
- How to approach other negotiations
- To negotiate conflict, including office politics
- To navigate failed negotiations
- Why your sisterhood is crucial for negotiations

How to get a pay rise

We started this chapter with how not to ask for a pay rise. So how do you do it effectively? As someone who has sat on the other side of the table, I know what works and what doesn't.

You need to prepare your business case. Start by working out what you've recently delivered for the company and whether/how your role has expanded. Are there further areas of responsibility you can take on? If you want a pay rise just because you've done a really great job, then you're going to have to prove it. What measurables can you talk about, either in terms of sales or clients you've brought in, or internal projects you've taken on? You need to make sure that you include your successes from the whole year, not just the most recent ones. A review needs to be evidence-based, so document your successes, detailing any extraneous circumstances, for example, 'I delivered a 5 per cent profit growth even though there was a market decline.'

Next, think about the amount you want. Do bear in mind that women typically under egg the amount they are asking for, but don't be unrealistic – that just looks like you don't know the sector. Go out and talk to recruiters to find out what other companies pay people in your position. What would you be happy to compromise on? Are there any other perks you could negotiate if money is off the table? After that you need to practise, practise, practise with someone who can play devil's advocate. Someone who can give you really harsh answers, so you know how to deal with them if they come up for real. A negotiation is almost always going to be on the edge of your comfort zone – you have to become comfortable feeling uncomfortable.

Once you feel ready to approach your boss, say, 'I want to make time with you to talk about my compensation. Over the last six months, I've delivered *XYZ* for the business and I'm looking to take on *ABC* responsibilities. I love working here, I'm here for the long term. Can we put in a time in the next week to discuss this further?' You are giving them a chance to think about it properly, rather than just cornering them in a general catch-up meeting.

But be prepared to negotiate there and then if they have the time. This is where your preparation comes in. If there's no extra money for your role, and sometimes there really isn't, then what else can you negotiate on? There's so much more to your compensation than just your pay packet. Other areas to think about include a bigger contribution into your pension or working flexibly, negotiating a bigger bonus percentage – which means that your performance is tied to the company, so should be a win-win – or even shares in the business. That's a hard one for a boss to turn down because it's no cost to the founders, and it proves that the employee is in it for the long term.

If you've got a genuine alternative job offer on the table that you're tempted to take because of the money, it's important to be honest about it. However, don't ever use leaving as an empty threat; in those instances, I always just think, 'Well, go.'

Try to keep emotion out of it. It's hard because pay is tied up with self-worth. Remember, this is a business negotiation which is where practice is essential. Either look in the mirror and put your game face on, or get someone in your work sisterhood to role-play with you again. If it's too hard to negotiate for yourself, imagine you're doing it for someone else: the favourite person in your team, your mum, your sister. It can really help.

Be precise with your figures (look back at chapter six for help) and assertive in your language (refer to chapter five), but don't forget to be charming and persuasive rather than aggressive and pushy.

And what if after this prep, and after doing all of the above, your boss listens to your case and says, 'I'll come back to you, I'll put some time in next month for us'? Try to (politely) resist. They don't need a month to think about it; schedule the follow-up meeting for the next week.

The final way to get more money? Get a new job. A study by McKinsey found that women early in their careers are less likely to get promoted than their male colleagues. Anna discovered that her way around this was to move about a lot early in her career. There's good reason for this: if you're a junior in a role and you're being paid £25,000, well, there's probably a cap on that role. Perhaps you can move up or sideways in your organisation – or indeed move to another company where you can get slightly further up the ladder with more money.

However, remember to commit to all the steps above when you're negotiating your starting salary. Once you sign on the dotted line somewhere new, you're unlikely to get another pay rise for a while.

Other money negotiations

A pay rise is a negotiation that contains so many lessons you can extrapolate for other negotiations you might encounter. Here are two other money-based examples you could experience in the workplace, and how to tackle them.

Negotiating sales deals

'Negotiation is a big part of sales,' Cassandra Stavrou, co-founder of Propercorn, says. 'But firstly, it's about a relationship, building a bit of rapport, and understanding each other's needs.' As with pay rises, Cassandra says that sales deals are not all about the price. It's down, yet again, to what you're prepared to give and take. 'There are other things you can offer that are of less value to you in terms of time and cost, but valuable to the other party, such as payment terms, promotional support or marketing.' Make sure you're clear on the whole landscape and what is valuable to the other person – it's the essence of all negotiation.

Raising investment

It's tough raising investment if you're a woman. The stats are against us: in both the US and the UK, in 2017 less than 2 per cent of venture capital funding went to female-led businesses. And while the stats are going up, women still need to fight twice as hard to get money. I've been on both sides of the table – someone asking for money and someone being asked to invest – and here are the three things that I think are essential:

1. Be able to demonstrate your business has traction. Before you approach professional investors, beg, borrow or steal from anyone you can to get your business going. Target friends and family for capital first, if you need it. Show that your idea works when you spend a little – and this makes it easier to think it will work tenfold when you have a lot.

2. When it comes to negotiating for investment, you have to take lots of the same steps as we have already rehearsed in this chapter. It's a negotiation after all. You need to do your homework so that you're ready to present data on why your business is worth X, the performance of your business, market opportunity and what competitors are being valued at. You need context of what you were once valued at and what you've done since then.

3. Forget everything you've seen on TV; negotiation is not always about being pushy. We've seen too many people come in who've read that they need to be confident, and they do – but not arrogant. The art of negotiation is a delicate dance and you've got to pick your moment.

Timing is everything. The first thing that turns me off is when people – often men – come in too aggressively with naïve presentations that exaggerate the potential for revenue and show 'hockey stick' growth without caveat. Just because the market potential is enormous it doesn't necessarily mean you'll go from £0 revenue in year one to £1 billion in year three – and believe me, some people seem to assume they will. Instead of being impressive, it reveals a complete lack of credibility. Be ambitious, be passionate, but be backable.

Negotiating conflict

It's not just when talking money where you need to sharpen your negotiating skills. Office politics can require you to deploy your best negotiation skills. Business – as in the rest of life – attracts a wide range of personalities and throws you all together into a melting pot. Anna and I certainly have to deal with some complicated people in our work lives. 'The more diverse the set of people talking, the more you can get into a situation of tension,' WPP's Karen Blackett says.

Conflict itself isn't something to shy away from, as I think many women do. Men often seem to thrive on it. Karen actually thinks conflict is a good thing: 'The end result will be better because you have considered all viewpoints. Even if it doesn't go your way, you can at least know that you have been heard.'

When you're approaching a tough conversation, it's important that your intention is to have a dialogue, rather than a rant, that you want to resolve positively and treat each other with respect. For that to happen, ideally you need to set aside the right time and place to have a meaningful discussion.

Karen advises, 'In a conflict situation, remember that all the other person wants to know is that you have heard their point.' She says that you don't necessarily need to agree with what they're saying, but you do need to value and respect it. An effective way to convey this is to repeat back what they have said to indicate you are listening carefully. Use this to calm the conversation down and move away from the conflict. You can use questioning to clarify the different viewpoints being shared. If these strategies don't work, it's perhaps best to stop the conversation and revisit it later on. 'You want to leave the conversation feeling good, not beaten up.'

Anna has had experience of this at work; she's had bosses who love conflict, who have shouted, screamed and hit their fists on tables. As a result, she's incredibly good at keeping calm and defusing a situation. It's her special power. When someone is shouting, they are probably out of control, so your options to respond are to be cowed, fight fire with fire, or defuse it. If you can do the latter, then you're the one in control and that's a very powerful position.

Defusing can be a challenge – and it takes practice – but try to listen to the nuggets of truth that are hidden in the rant. There's often something buried in there that's fair, and if you can address that, you might win them over. The worst thing you can be is defensive as that adds fuel to the fire. And while it's tempting to say nothing and to weather the storm, resist that option because that's passive behaviour. It's about getting the measure right.

I'm worse than Anna at keeping schtum. If someone comes at me, I have to work hard not to go at them because

I'm punchy. So, it's essential that you have someone in your sisterhood who you can rehearse with for moments like these.

Handling bullies

Part of negotiating office politics is learning how to handle bullies, who, according to a survey by workplacebullying.org, particularly target women, who made up about two-thirds of their targets. The retail consultant and broadcaster Mary Portas has spoken about how she was bullied by a male boss: 'He would do things like take the rest of the team out for lunch, where they would discuss projects that I was involved in, deliberately leaving me out of the process.'

She advises calling it out. 'So often, women in business think they're causing a situation by speaking up,' she has said. 'They're not. It's about being open and honest, which is vital to how we work.'

I've seen this in meetings when men speak over women. Facebook's Nicola Mendelsohn says she's witnessed this, too. 'It's so common when men interrupt and speak over the top of women and don't listen to the point they were trying to make. That's a terrible thing to happen. Men and women can work together really well,' she says. 'We just have to create space for everyone.' The work sisterhood has to step up in these instances.

Queen Bee syndrome

Statistics say it's mainly men who will be the workplace bullies (70 per cent of the time), but women are capable of it too. The Queen Bee syndrome was identified by social psychologist Carol Tavris and two colleagues in 1974. It described an 'anti-feminist woman' who was at the top of an organisation who had made it against the odds, and who resented helping women coming up behind her – because in the 1970s the business world really was a man's world.

It was largely dismissed as just the result of there being too few women at the top, and that women were therefore naturally pitted against each other. But it's a topic that has been reignited by Cecilia Harvey, a businesswoman and entrepreneur who recently wrote a research paper where she interviewed 100 senior women and found that most of them had experienced bullying at work by women. It's not something that I've personally experienced, but Anna definitely did early in her career. She talks about a female boss who belittled her. She recognised quite quickly that she would be unable to work with her long term and, despite the fact that she loved her job, that she would need to move on to realise her potential. It was the right thing to do. Her next move allowed her to progress into a much more senior role, and along her path to CEO and then onwards to join the entrepreneurial circus at AllBright with me. Sometimes the best negotiation tactic is to cut and run.

Emotions at work

Handling your emotions at work can sometimes be part of a negotiation – and it's a topic that can often be problematic for women. There have been reams written about this issue and people come down on both sides of the argument. Some say that crying at work is healthy and authentic. We're on the other side of the argument. We feel that crying is as bad as shouting and fist thumping – it shows you're out of control, which as a leader is a weak position to occupy.

We're all human and emotions can take us all by surprise – usually when something else is happening in your personal life. Anna admits to having cried at work (just once): she was heavily pregnant and totally unexpectedly her most trusted lieutenant handed in her notice. It's fair enough to blame her hormones in that situation! But on the whole, if you feel like you're going to cry, try to go somewhere private – make any excuse to get yourself out of there. This is where it's crucial that you rely on a supportive peer network. Literally phone a friend and rant, moan and cry to them in private – not in the office.

If you're on the other end of tears – or anger – in the office, you just have to say, 'You're very upset, let's take time out.' Emotions can get the better of us all, and it's not only a kindness to postpone the discussion, but it will result in a better negotiation for everyone.

Failures in negotiations

Having spent a chapter discussing how to succeed at negotiations, it's vital to say that there are times when they don't work out. Deals fall off the table, you feel you're compromising too far, or that investor turns you down (and of course, all of this happens to us and will keep on happening). If you've done everything that you can, then don't beat yourself up. It could just be the wrong timing, in which case you have to try again at a different point. Sometimes it's just simply the wrong deal. The important thing is you tried. 'Even if it doesn't go your way, and you don't get the result you want, you can come away knowing that you put your point across,' Karen Blackett says. 'It's really important that your voice is heard and that you do go into those situations.' The more you negotiate, the more confident you'll get and the better you'll become.

CASE STUDY: SUE WILLIAMS, HOSTAGE NEGOTIATOR

Think you've faced a tough negotiation? Well, spare a thought for Sue Williams, a hostage negotiator who worked for the Metropolitan Police for 27 years and now works for humanitarian charities to secure the release of kidnapped staff abroad. 'The negotiations I've been involved with have saved hundreds of lives,' she says.

She has and continues to work on cases of kidnappings, suicide prevention, sieges and crimes including bank robberies.

But whether you're talking down a warlord with an AK-47 or brokering a business deal, she says there are strategies that work for both. 'There are some common mistakes lots of people make during negotiations,' she says. 'The biggest is that we all have an agenda in our heads, and you want and expect the other person to stick to that – they don't always. Or we're so busy thinking about the next move or formulating our reply that we don't actively listen to the other person. The reason we're not very good at listening sometimes is that we presume we know what the other person is going to say, so we jump to our conclusions.'

If your negotiation is met with a what she terms 'hostile silence', she advises you to keep cool. 'Don't fill silence with gabbling,' she says. Instead, 'You could try a direct question to force a reply, such as, "what are you thinking about?" or, "have I stunned you?".'

Another common mistake, she says, is that we often set our own deadlines in an attempt to seem efficient, such as saying 'I'll get back to you in 20 minutes'. 'You need to just pause and think, "do I need to do that?" You don't necessarily know how long it will take you and you are adding extra pressure on yourself.'

Like us, Sue says that preparation is the key to a successful negotiation. 'When you see people doing my job in the movies they just turn up and start talking. That's Hollywood, but not real life,' she says. 'You have to start preparing way before you start communicating. You have to earn the right to negotiate.' It means knowing what is negotiable, and what your fallback plan is, too.

Which means research on your counterpart, their organisation and all the other stakeholders. 'You've got to think, "who else has got a dog in this race?" Managing the stakeholders – such as the parents of abducted children – is sometimes harder than managing the kidnapper, she says. Translated to the boardroom, that could be anxious bosses or shareholders. 'Other stakeholders can say the wrong thing at the wrong point if you're not prepared.'

Which can include yourself. 'You've absolutely got to leave your preconceptions at the door,' she says. 'We've all got unconscious bias – as long as you understand what yours is, you can deal with it. But you have to filter out any bad experiences and go in with an open mind.'

CHAPTER RECAP: The Art Of Negotiation

The essence of negotiation: There are some key rules for all negotiations. Do your homework, be prepared and practise with a friend or work sister. Know that all negotiations involve give and take, and that you need to be ready to concede in areas.

Negotiating a pay rise: Remember to make a business case for your pay rise. Research what others in your sector are paid and clearly state your case. Aim high, but don't be unrealistic.

Raising investment: It is statistically harder for women to get investment, so we have to work harder at the negotiating table. Know every figure about your business and its market position. Remember that negotiating is a dance and timing is everything.

Negotiating conflict: In most conflict situations, remember that really all the other person wants to know is that you have heard their point. If they are ranting and out of control, then stay calm, present the facts and try to listen out for some nuggets of truth.

Handling bullies: Bullies are a fact of life; you either have to learn how to negotiate with them and handle them to your advantage or see the situation for what it is and get out.

Emotions at work: We don't think the workplace is the right environment to express tears or anger: it shows a person out of control and that's not inspiring leader material. Try hard to keep your emotions in check.

Failures in negotiations: If you've done all you can by preparing, practising and dancing the negotiation dance and it doesn't work out – well, that's life. Not all deals work out. Dust yourself off, and try another time. The more you practise negotiating, the better you get.

WORKSHEET: SMASHING NEGOTIATIONS

Identify an upcoming negotiation, do your homework: get clear on the ideal and minimum outcome needed and plan your approach.

Ask yourself:

a) What is the desired outcome from the negotiation?

_____

_____

_____

_____

b) What do you know about the other person and the circumstances surrounding each issue?

Person:

_____

_____

_____

_____

Circumstances:

_____

_____

_____

_____

c) What are the issues you're prepared to concede on and what is your line in the sand?

Concede:

_____

_____

_____

_____

Stick:

_____

_____

_____

_____

During the negotiations, remember to stay confident, be flexible and try to enjoy the experience! Afterwards, reflect on what went well, what didn't and how you can use this to become a more skilled negotiator in future.

CHAPTER ELEVEN

A World-class Hustler

'In the middle of difficulty lies opportunity'

Albert Einstein

Debbie

The hustle is something that women can feel embarrassed about; perhaps because it sounds a bit grubby. But what lots of people underestimate is that business *is* grubby! A lot of the hustle is, quite frankly, about following the money. That sounds blunt and unromantic, but that really is the fundamental essence of business. For me, the hustle is about dogged hard work and persistence, spotting and following up opportunities in any way you can and taking risks. Inevitably, at the start at least, it can also mean working out who might be useful to you and asking people for favours. I've been hustling since I was 25 and I'm happy to own that, although the way I do it now has changed. But the hustle, at its heart, is about making things happen for yourself. 'You have to believe in yourself and be a driver,' coordinating producer Sandy Nunez agrees. 'You can't wait for people to offer you chances.'

If you're hustling, you're putting yourself and your ideas out there, and that can be scary. This is where you need to draw on the lessons we've talked about through the book – confidence strategies from chapter three, and your carefully crafted personal brand, practised elevator pitch from chapter five and communication style from chapter six. And get ready to get into a negotiation on the spot – skills you just learned in chapter ten. The hustle employs all of these skills and tactics, and you have to get ready to use them – as well as, of course, to lean on a killer sisterhood who can help connect you to the right people and opportunities.

A lot of women in particular, I've found, plan their business journey as a linear path, but in reality, growth and amazing opportunities often come from the curve balls that present themselves. Sometimes you just need to chase after them. If you're a good hustler, you're able to adapt and change quickly, recognising when you need to drop things and when you need to push. It means that your business almost never ends up being the thing that you started with, because you couldn't foresee the opportunities that have arisen, and you have to be OK with that. As Joy Mangano, the queen of home shopping, with over $3 billion in sales of products like the Miracle Mop, has said: 'Know that you can shift your skis – it's never too early or too late to take that path.'

I've found this to be very true. When I was CEO of Love Home Swap, we thought hard about where our business sat and who it would be of interest to. We realised that online home rentals were essentially the digital future of timeshare companies, a market whose ageing audience was declining. And so, we made sure that we had a presence at the big global timeshare conferences. It was there that I got to know Wyndham, who eventually acquired the business. I didn't go with any intention of making a big sale, but while I was there

I realised there was an opportunity, and I made my introductions. It was a long deal with multiple negotiations, but selling the business to them three years later had its roots in that moment of hustle.

The hustle is about operating in the weeds – by which I mean making those calls to suppliers yourself, getting your product on the shelf by any means possible, or that foot in the door of a corporation. A danger arises when people feel too grand to do the small things in life. As Georgia Louise – the facialist with a remarkable story of how her relentless hustle got her from being an 18-year-old with rented beauty rooms to the point where she is known as one of the best aestheticians in America, who we profile at the end of the chapter – says, 'No one else can pick up that phone but you, if you want to get in the door you're the one who has to make that call. The more calls you make, the better you get at it.' We know we've spoken about the importance of delegation as you scale, but at any moment in your business journey you need to be prepared to do anything yourself to make you or your business a success.

It's also true that as circumstances change, so does the way you hustle. When I was starting out, I had very little to offer anyone in return for the favours I was asking. But I've made it my mission throughout my career since then to always be as generous as I can with my connections and, where I can, time. These days (compared to when I was starting out), I have better connections and more to offer in return. My hustle now is less about scrabbling around and asking for favours, and more around my work ethic, taking risks, thinking hard how to use connections and being audacious. But I still hustle every day. You need persistence, you need charm and you need a network. Plus, a dollop of luck.

What you'll learn in this chapter:

- How to spot an opportunity
- To be a 'salespreneur'
- To practise the art of persistence
- Why you also hustle inside a corporation
- How to use your network to hustle

Sniffing out the opportunity

Kelly Hoppen's first big break, as she described in chapter five, was designing a family friend's kitchen – this allowed her to show off her work, her network expanded and it snowballed from there. 'From day one, when given the opportunity to design without much experience, I just went for it and learned very quickly along the way,' she says. 'You have to have confidence and belief in your ability.'

How to spot an opportunity? Lynda Gratton, professor of management practice at London Business School and author of *The Shift*, says that curiosity is absolutely key. 'You have to remain curious,' she says, 'about events, people, the world you live in. Keep travelling and keep your eyes open, try to understand how things work. That for me has been an enormous key to my success.'

A great example of this is Beatriz Acevedo's career transformation. Beatriz was an Emmy-award winning TV host and writer for a Mexican network when she realised that other young Latinos born in the US were not consuming the traditional Spanish language TV content that was available to them. In response, she set up her own digital media company 'to really target them, serve content and also to open doors and create opportunity for the next generation of filmmakers'.

Strike while the iron's hot

Once you've identified the opportunity, you have to follow through. 'I think every single person is surrounded by opportunities,' Anastasia Soare says, 'but you need to be ready to see it, grab it, and then do something with it.' Even if that means accepting something that you're not entirely sure you can do – if you work hard enough, you will be able to. Sandy Nunez is particularly passionate about this. When she was asked to join *SportsCenter* as coordinating producer, and one of the few women at the top of sports broadcasting, she recounts, 'They said on a scale of one to ten, how's your sport's knowledge? I wanted the job so I said eight. Actually, it was more like a two.' We want more women to go for it like this.

Sell, sell, sell

One skill I have developed over time is the ability to make the most out of every chance meeting – and to capitalise on every potential connection.

To be a good hustler you have to have your strategic brain switched on the whole time because you never know who you'll meet. To be a world-class hustler, you always need to be ready to sell your idea and yourself. We've talked about the importance of knowing your personal brand and having your elevator pitch ready, and this is why: because you never know who you're in a room with. Some of the most extraordinary things have happened to us because we've accidentally found ourselves in a certain situation. It can be anywhere, from an unlikely business conference to a wedding where you're sitting on a table with someone you think might be useful to you. From there, you need to quickly work out how to maximise your conversation.

In 2017, I was introduced to a very well-known chairman by a headhunter who wanted to talk about me joining one of his boards. When I was chatting to him, I realised that I wanted to talk about AllBright more than I wanted to talk about the opportunity on the table. So, I turned the conversation round into me recruiting him. (He is now our non-executive chairman at AllBright.)

It's an example of what Julia Hobsbawm, entrepreneur and author, calls being a 'salespreneur'. 'I like selling, I always have liked the art of communication and persuasion,' she says. She cautions that there is a 'but' to this: you still need the self-awareness that we discussed in chapter five. 'It is not good if you are unable to notice if someone actually wants what you are selling: that would be a misjudgement.' It's a fine line.

Tap into your confidence

I think women can often feel embarrassed about the hustle – Anna definitely found it hard at first when she was suddenly hustling for herself, rather than on behalf of a corporation. It's tough putting yourself, your ideas and your business out there in the wider world and pitching for work, or asking for favours, or whatever way you have to hustle, especially as women are brought up being told not to be too grabby. But you have to put your game face on, make your pitch and, just as we spoke about making a business case for a pay rise in the last chapter, present how your offer will benefit the other person. Perhaps it's financial, perhaps its through building relationships, or perhaps it's just goodwill in the bank! You have to believe in your product and yourself. It's all about confidence. But even if you are naturally lacking in it personally, and remember in chapter three we said that it's a very common female trait, you can still have confidence in your product or business and let that drive you forward.

Laurie Nouchka, an artist who also designs activewear for clients including Soho House and Equinox, agrees. She says she finds confidence in knowing that her product and brand are answering a *need* for others. 'In my mind, I see gaps in something, or opportunities to suggest an idea and I have no fear in reaching out to people,' she says. 'I like to offer a creative solution to problems or gaps I think people sometimes don't see. I'm unafraid to talk about ideas and unafraid to try and make them happen. I think the combination of those means people sense that and want to work with you.' She's absolutely right: your product, business or service is actually helpful to someone else.

That's not to say you should be bullish. We've had meetings with people who have walked in with a too-hard sell; we joke that they've watched too many episodes of *Dragons' Den*. As *Slay in Your Lane* author Elizabeth Uviebinené advises, 'You do need to walk into a meeting and be secure in the knowledge that you have, but also remember you don't know everything. You need to be open to new skills, people and ideas.' So don't connect the hustle with everything you see on television – remember that humility and curiosity are seductive qualities. We always say you catch more flies with honey than vinegar.

The art of persistence

To be successful you have to have enough force of personality and charm without driving people completely mad. You need to be convincing and have your facts ready and presentable, and then be ready to follow up on your pitch. And for that, persistence is key. Olivia Wollenberg, founder of Livia's Kitchen, has a brilliant story about her hustle, showing just how persistence can pay off: 'When I launched the company, I wasn't getting anywhere with emails to buyers – they just ignored me. So, I turned up to their offices with my crumbles. When I delivered my products to *Vogue*, they put them up on their Instagram feed and I got my first 3,000 followers. It was at that point that I finally got buyers to listen to me – by showing them *Vogue*'s endorsement. Getting in front of people is the hard job when you start out, so you have to constantly think about new ways to make that happen.'

There's no doubt she's a success now, but four years on she hasn't stopped hustling. 'I don't do any less hustling four years on than I did when I launched the company,' she laughs. 'I am still constantly knocking on doors and making sure I am getting our product in front of the right people.' It's that approach that will keep her star rising.

Liv Little, founder of the successful growing gal-dem brand, says, 'I'm used to reaching out and having stuff not work. I've realised you have to throw a lot of stuff out and hope it sticks. You have to be persistent.'

You need persistence – and inner confidence – to keep going when people around you tell you your idea isn't worthwhile, which believe me, people do all the time. Julia has had experience of this. When she set up her content and connection organisation, Editorial Intelligence, in 2005, just as Facebook was beginning to rise in popularity, 'people laughed in my face and in print about [my idea] to have a business modelled on face-to-face in a Facebook world,' she says. 'But I persevered.' She has had the last laugh: historian Simon Schama describes her as 'the wizard of modern connection'.

Don't be put off by rejection

This leads on to not accepting 'no' for an answer. It's really easy to hear a 'no' and immediately retreat: they don't like you or your idea. But the best hustlers keep going. Joy Mangano says, 'Don't be afraid of hearing no – no is just the beginning. I hear more no's today; it's [just] a matter of how do I shift that into a yes. That's a start of something else.'

Elizabeth Uviebiné agrees that for her, 'No's just mean not now.' When she and Yomi Adegoke approached women that they wanted to feature in their book, initially they did so when they didn't have a publisher. 'So, if we got a no, we thought when we do have a publisher, we can approach them again and turn that no into a yes.' Which is exactly what they did.

She's absolutely right – timing is everything. I've had ideas that have 'failed' because the market hasn't been right, or people's expectations are not there yet. It doesn't stop me trying. Facialist Georgia Louise agrees: 'Be prepared for people to tell you you won't succeed; I've had so many people tell me that – but be bold and brave in your vision.' We've had it too; people were sniffy to say the least about our idea for a women's club, but the feedback from our members has more than proved we were right. We've had women members talk to us with tears in their eyes, explaining how simply having a space and a supportive environment, with the opportunity to meet like-minded women, has ignited their own business dreams. That is all the validation we need.

Hustling in a corporation

While the hustle is most associated with the entrepreneurial world, it applies just as much to those in corporations. When Anna was a CEO, she would say at most board meetings, 'Don't forget, we are a commercial organisation and everything's for sale.' Her story of one her most successful hustles was when she met one of the board of Walmart-owned Asda, who was talking about how he wished the content for their instore magazine was better. As CEO of a string of glossy magazines, that might seem a strange crossover, but Anna responded by asking him whether her company could do the content for them. She had no idea how they would actually do it, but over a year later – remember what

I said about persistence – he got in touch to say he'd like to take her up on the offer, and she moved the company into third-party content production. It was a left-field move for a high-end brand business, but it soon became a very important revenue stream for the company. It's another reminder that you have to put yourself out there, even if you work for a big company.

How your network can help

Your personal network is absolutely crucial to the hustle, as Anna and I have both found. A lot of our friends were founding members and investors in AllBright, because they believed in us and the vision for the business. You also need your network to help you with connections – it's hard to sell an idea to someone you've never met and who has no association to you. We always advise not to go big on an ask over email to a stranger – they're probably not going to respond.

But you can let your product help boost your own network, as Laurie Nouchka found. 'I like to connect with people and reach out and build a community – which relates to all areas of my work,' she says. 'In the early days, the clothing did the talking – it was unique and caught people's eye – but I never wanted to just sell clothes. The "putting them out there" was just a vehicle to drive interest in my work and me and from there I built relationships.'

It's a two-way thing, though. You have to spend time building up connections and offering out favours before you need help, including opening up your network to others. There's always someone out there on the hustle.

CASE STUDY: GEORGIA LOUISE, FOUNDER OF
GEORGIA LOUISE

Georgia Louise is now regarded as the top facialist in America, with a client list boasting Hollywood A-listers including Linda Evangelista, Jennifer Lawrence, Sandra Bullock and Cate Blanchett. Georgia even made global headlines in 2018 after Cate credited her amazing glow to Georgia's $650 so-called 'penis' facial, which uses a radical serum called EGF, which is derived from new-born baby foreskin cells cloned in a lab!

It's an amusing headline that charts a career that started from nothing and has been driven by pure hustle. After training as a facialist in high-end spas, Georgia started her own business when she was 18 in a rented basement. She had no clients of her own, so would go up to the hairdresser's a floor above and try to sweet talk their customers. One client became five clients – they would refer their friends.' She was a huge success, with well-heeled clients that included the British royal family and Chelsea It girls. But two years after she started, the landlord sold the building, and because of the amount she had invested in advanced facial machines – intending to pay off the debt as her business grew – she was left having to declare herself bankrupt. 'I sat on a park bench for hours thinking, what am I going to do? It was a harsh lesson to learn.'

Because UK law forbids people owning businesses for a year after bankruptcy, Georgia decided to become a trainer on specialist facial microcurrent machines for the company CACI International. 'It was a really good opportunity,' she says. 'I did really well for myself, but my heart wasn't in it – I missed my business.'

Eventually the clock ran down and she had saved up enough money to start again. She rented another room and started hustling again. 'It was hard. Some of my clients stuck with me, but I had to go up to the salon upstairs and hustle clients again. It worked: 18 months later she needed to rent more space.

On the side, she formulated her own product range in her kitchen, and invited over Nicky Kinnaird, founder of the boutique beauty store Space NK, who was impressed. 'I really wanted to be stocked by Space NK.' Sure enough, she was.

At that point, she met an American man (who would later become her husband), fell in love and moved to New York. 'So, I had to start again – again. But once you've done it twice before, you know you can do it. I had the drive and determination not to fail.'

In the first week of moving there, before Georgia had the chance to set up shop, her old employer CACI called her. 'They said, "We have a client who has her own machine; it's broken and we need you to go and repair it." I rocked up at the house and it was [supermodel] Linda Evangelista's house! She was having a private Pilates lesson and pointed to the machine in the corner. I was sweating buckets as I tried to fix it, but it worked – thank God.' She told Linda the good news, and also reminded her how to use the probes, 'which she said no one had explained properly before; so, I suggested she lie down and I show her.' It was a masterstroke of spotting an opportunity and going for it. An hour and a half later, Linda asked Georgia to come back the next day, and she became her first – and a regular – client. From there, Linda introduced Georgia to Gucci Westman, then the creative director at Revlon, who then forwarded her details to her star-studded address book, including Cameron Diaz and Drew Barrymore – 'this A-list clientele I'd never had before'.

Thus, the third incarnation of her business was born. After doing facials in clients' apartments and then renting a space below an acupuncturist, she now owns the lease on her 16,000sq ft treatment space on Manhattan's Upper East Side. She's fully booked and is widely regarded as the best facialist in America. 'All my success is down to two things,' she says. 'The hustle that I've always had to do throughout my career and the power of female networks. I couldn't have succeeded without either.'

CHAPTER RECAP: A World-class Hustler

Hustle takes time to craft and perfect, but once you do, you'll reap the career rewards.

Opportunity: You have to be always alert to an opportunity. Not everyone walks into a supermodel's home, but there are always extra projects you could volunteer for, or connections to follow up.

Selling: You always need to be ready to sell your idea and yourself. Your strategic brain should always be switched on and your elevator pitch ready because you never know who you'll meet.

Confidence: Embarrassment over hustling comes down, in part, to lack of confidence. Remember why you're doing this (your motivations and goals) and what you've got to offer.

Persistence: Some deals or opportunities can take years to come to fruition. You also need persistence – and inner confidence – to keep going when people around you tell you your idea isn't worthwhile.

Ignoring rejection: A true hustler isn't put off by a 'no'; it could just mean that it's not the right time and you should try again later, or in a slightly different way. You have to figure out how to turn that 'no' into a 'yes'.

Hustling inside corporations: The art of the hustle applies just as much to those in corporations. The key to promotion is to be keen and on the hunt for opportunities.

Network: Your personal network is absolutely crucial to the hustle. But you have to spend time before you need help building up connections and offering out favours. Always think what your ask is, and what you can offer in return.

WORKSHEET: TURNING A NO INTO A YES

Rejection happens to all of us and it can feel wounding. But the best hustlers learn to shrug off the hurt feelings and work out how to turn that no into a yes. Think about something you've recently asked for where you were either turned down outright, or didn't get a firm yes. Did the person give a reason why? Can you think of any other reasons? For example, is the market right, is your timing right, was your pitch perfect, is your business case solid, did you target the right person in the company, did you go in with a big ask to a stranger without any prior connection? Consider all the factors and give it another go. Good luck.

The ask: _____

Reasons given for the rejection (if any):

_____

_____

_____

_____

Other factors you think might be applicable:

_____

_____

_____

_____

How you can tweak your pitch:

_____

_____

_____

_____

CHAPTER TWELVE

Sisterhood Works

'For some reason I have better luck when I work with women. I guess I have a good sense of sisterhood'

Dolly Parton

Anna

There are some women you meet whom you instantly fall in love with. It's hard to underestimate the positive momentum that comes from women supporting and inspiring each other. It's no exaggeration to say that my career has been transformed in so many ways by meeting my work best friend, Debbie. Since we met we've had each other's backs, empowering and improving each other. We're really good at building on each other's strengths and ideas and believing in each other in the challenging times. As Michelle Obama says in *Becoming*, 'Find people who'll make you better.' We both did that.

We both had strong work sisterhoods before we met, and we credit them with getting us to the top of our respective fields. We know other high-powered women who say the same – including many of the women on these pages, like Anastasia Soare, who says, 'Networks are crucial – I owe my career to so many incredible women, including clients and people who supported me from early on.' Or Pam Kaufman, president of Viacom Nickelodean Global Consumer Products, who says that 'female networks have been *instrumental* to my success'. But this is not just anecdotal; we conducted research into the topic and found that the higher up women were in an organisation, the more likely they were to have a broad sisterhood. The findings totally backed up our own experience: sisterhood works.

This book has been guiding you through the principals that we think will supercharge your career, from working out your goals and establishing your motivations, to building up your confidence, and practical steps like working on your business model and negotiation tactics. Developing a work sisterhood is crucial every step of the way. Not just as a support network to get through the tough times, but to help you be better, to work out a game plan, and to workshop and practise everything you need to help you climb each rung of the career ladder.

Women's networks have long existed. In America, the women's club movement began in the mid nineteenth century with the aim of providing women with an independent avenue for education and active community service; in 1915 the Women's Institute was formed in the UK. Fast forward to now, and never has the idea of female sisterhood been more powerful: we've seen it celebrated in pop culture with Beyoncé's lyrics of female empowerment and Taylor Swift's girl squad.

But we need to step it up a gear and use our considerable united power to enact further change. Even in 2019, there is a lack of women at the top in business. This is the entire *raison d'être* for AllBright, with the mission to celebrate and champion women to inspire change. We want our members' clubs to offer the support and networking opportunities that have been available to men for centuries through gentlemen's clubs and the old-boy networks.

The problem, up until now, is that while women are brilliant at forging connections in our personal lives, we don't necessarily do the same at work. Expanding networks to include a diverse range of views and voices as well as sectors and experience is absolutely key to helping us all learn and improve. 'The way that we change is working with people who are different to us and provide new role models,' says Lynda Gratton, who was a pioneer in her field, being one of the first female professors at London Business School. 'I always try to have friendships and associate with people who are very different from me.'

Networking is vital to getting your work sisterhood together. The thought of 'networking' can perhaps seem intimidating, until you realise that it's mutually beneficial: you've got as much to offer the other person as she has to you. It's a conversation and exchange of ideas and knowledge. You can network anywhere – in the gym, at a party, or online – although we'd argue you need to turn online relationships into real-world meets to truly maximise their potential.

We are out and proud feminists and our whole ethos is to celebrate and champion women, but unlike some other female-only endeavours, we have always been inclusive of men in our mission. Why? Because we have both found that what we term 'enlightened men' have been essential to our success. At AllBright's women's clubs, men are allowed in as guests of our female members, because we believe we need men to work with us on the journey. As our community of amazing women grows each day, we hope we can also continue to count on the support of enlightened men. To drive that change, we need to maximise the power of the sisterhood.

What you'll learn in this chapter:

- How to build your sisterhood
- Why diversity is important
- The different types of networks and how to navigate into them
- How to maintain your networks
- How to appoint a personal board of directors

Building your sisterhood

You know by now how vital we think a sisterhood is to success and in every step of your career. A strong network is something Debbie and I have found just keeps getting more essential as we get more experienced. You need different networks at different times, especially at times of big life change, like starting a business or having a baby (they often are described in the same terms!). But how do you build up your own supportive sisterhood?

Consider who is already in your gang

The best place to start is with the people you've known for years. I find that its my oldest friends – the ones who know me better than anyone else – who give me the most direct feedback and advice that really cuts through and makes me stop and think. Likewise, Lynda Gratton says one of her key advisors is a schoolfriend. 'I recently celebrated 50 years of friendship with one of my dearest friends who I was at school with,' she says. 'Those people who have been with you through your whole life [are] an extraordinary gift. I teach that to my MBA students.' It's vital to nurture those relationships, as they are the people who know you the best and who can often read you like a book.

After decades of research on networks and social health, Julia Hobsbawm has developed a model she calls 'hexagon thinking', and she suggests you create a 'social six' team around you. She says that her husband Alaric and their 18-year-old daughter Anoushka are the two family members she confides in and takes counsel from most. Outside that, she has 'four amazing women' that form the basis of her sisterhood: one friend who she has known for 30 years and whose 'judgement is the most sound of anyone I know', as well as three newer work sisters who are, she says, 'kind, wise and generous'.

Look around at who you already have supporting you – they are your sisterhood.

Look for diversity of opinion

Friends, family and work colleagues are a great leaping-off point when building your sisterhood, but you need to be cautious of surrounding yourself with different versions of you. Diversity of opinion, experience and sector knowledge is important.

The *Sunday Times*'s Lorraine Candy found that while older, more experienced colleagues are helpful, she has found enormous value in including younger women in her sisterhood, too. 'I have actually learned as much from really junior women in business as I have from powerful decision makers,' she says.

Lorraine also says that she tries to move outside of her usual circles, in order to increase the range of people she meets. 'I will often decline fashion or beauty events but attend events in other related industries. It is always good to meet new people in other areas and find out how they work.'

We have both been conscious of building up diverse networks. We already come from different industries and have different backgrounds and former colleagues, but another key area of diversity for us is including men in our sisterhood. Because we've both had fantastic male support, from bosses, investors, business partners and chairmen along the way who have been instrumental in our success. I couldn't have reached the position of CEO without the help from the men in my professional life, and most of the investors in AllBright are men. They believe in our mission and they are prepared to support us as we realise it. I also couldn't have achieved my career aspirations to date without the amazing support of the men in my personal life – notably my husband and my son, but also my hugely encouraging male friends.

The truth is we operate in a world where we coexist with men and the power balance still rests with them, so the only way we achieve real change is to make it happen together. Many men recognise that women make their businesses better and promote women to top jobs – as is my experience. There are lots of enlightened men out there who are keen to support the sisterhood and the more that join their ranks the better. Make sure you include the best men in your sisterhood.

How to chat to people from different industries

If you're putting yourself out there and trying to network with people from different industries, it can feel daunting if you don't *exactly* understand what they do. My tactic is to ask people to describe a typical day or week and to break down what percentage of their time they spend on which activities. Most people don't think about this too often, as they just have their heads down doing their jobs. If you give them time to think about the response carefully, you can get a really good idea of what a role entails. You might, for example, think a role like a communications director is all about wining and dining the media and coming up with great creative ideas, when in fact someone in that role might spend most of their time pitching for new business or doing account administration. The other way to try and understand what's involved in someone's role is to ask them what their top three priorities are. Again, this gives you an idea of the scope of their role and the issues they face.

Find a mentor

Mentors are key members of your sisterhood. They're the people who are looking out for you and can advise you, especially earlier in your career. Having someone telling you to go for it and backing you is a huge confidence boost.

Studies back this up, showing that people who ask for advice from managers about how to advance are more likely to get promoted. SoulCycle's Melanie Whelan discovered this, too: 'I've been fortunate to have a few women for whom I've worked who have invested deeply and personally in me to make sure I had a clear and meaningful path ahead of me. My first female boss saw something in me and promoted me before I was ready, gave me more responsibility than I deserved and, as a result, I achieved far more than I ever thought was possible. It was a turning point in my career, and I'll always be thankful for her belief in me.'

Yet women are statistically less likely to have someone mentoring them – so we think it's someone you should add to your gang. It doesn't have to be a formal relationship, or with someone who has done exactly what you've done, rather someone you respect who can help guide you.

How do you approach a mentor? Debbie is incredibly generous with her time to fellow female entrepreneurs and gets approached a lot. She explains that due to the volume of requests that she receives, it's often those with a personal connection that she follows up with, rather than total strangers. Using your network is crucial. It's good to be clear about what you want from a mentor, too. Their time is precious, so instead of telling your life story, make sure you are specific and outline what you want from them.

Different ways to network

If you have gaps to fill, then you'll need to network. The key to effective networking, as you build up your sisterhood, is about recognising that you need lots of amazing and varied women in all aspects of your life, and they – we – are everywhere. As you'll come to see, there is potential to network everywhere, from the gym changing rooms (Debbie has been approached here) to the school run to a friend's party (where Debbie and I met). If networking fills you with fear, reframe the concept in your mind. You just need to be curious about everyone you meet and the opportunities they could present to you, and how you can help them in return.

Just as with negotiations, networking is about give and take. Most people will be charmed and flattered by your interest in them. If you're keen to expand your network, say yes to all kinds of invitations – you don't know who you'll meet.

Official networking events

Let's start with the most dreaded type of networking: the official networking event. Trust us when we say, almost no one loves them. Baroness Tanni Grey-Thompson, the multiple Paralympic gold-medal winner has said: 'What I hate most is a cocktail reception. I always think I won't know anybody, that no one will talk to me, and it's going to be awful. But I make myself go and talk to people I don't know. It's good to put yourself in situations where you expose yourself to things that scare you.'

I often feel the same, but when you boil it down, it's not really that scary. You have to reframe the situation in your mind. It is not about having to make banter with the whole room; instead focus, as I do, on one or two people and really make the effort to connect with them. Ask people questions, while sharing stories from your personal life – your family, your interests, where you've been on holiday – they are all just ways of finding common ground. Professor Lynda Gratton says curiosity is the key: 'I go in and say, "Hi, tell me what you're interested in." I let my curiosity play the main role.'

It can be daunting walking into networking situations if they are rooms filled with men in suits (as they often are). We usually gravitate to the other women first. Debbie and I recently went to an event the Prime Minister was holding for the UK business community and, out of a sea of suits, we saw a handful of women in attendance. They came across to talk to us and the next thing we knew we were being photographed with the Prime Minister for the official image to promote the event. As we said in chapter five on personal branding, it's worth remembering that standing out can be an advantage!

There are techniques you learn in order to get the most out of these sorts of situations. 'I am terrible at small talk,' Lorraine Candy confesses. 'But if I am at an event or in a place with women I want to see more of, I do my research. I find out how they relax outside work, if they have a pet, or what their hobbies are and try to find common ground for authentic chat.'

That kind of background research is essential, especially if you're feeling nervous. Another good tip is to ask open-ended questions, rather than ones that can be answered with a yes or a no, as well as deploying your active listening skills from chapter five. Repeating back something someone has just said, especially if it's a complex description of their job or business, can serve to demonstrate you're listening, while you get a handle on what to say next. And while it can be tempting to quickly fill silences, don't. Take a minute. The other person will usually start talking, taking the pressure off you.

It's really important to give whoever you're talking to your undivided attention; we've all been in situations where the person you're having a conversation with is looking over your shoulder, assessing who else is worthy of their time. You have to make that person feel like they are the most important person in the room.

'At a networking event, I usually head to the bar since that is where most people are congregating and it's a great spot to start a conversation,' Pam Kaufman says. 'Since it's a "networking event", people are generally ready to meet others, so I literally extend my hand and introduce myself. To get the most out of the situation, I try to have as many "meaningful" conversations as possible by limiting my conversations to 10–15 minutes, and I always ask for a business card and follow up with an email within 24 hours.'

It's great advice, but what can be challenging is extracting yourself from a conversation, especially if you're a people pleaser. I've had to learn how to end conversations in a polite and friendly way and move on, without feeling embarrassed about it – otherwise you can be stuck talking to one person all evening. The best tip I've found is just to be confident about winding the conversation down and saying, 'It's been fascinating meeting you, thank you for the chat.' And moving on.

There can be other challenges to these kinds of events, aside from confidence issues. Author and academic Sinéad

Burke says she finds them hard because they are physically designed so that 'everyone stands up. Because of my physical disability, not only can they not hear me, but I can't hear them; I'm often talking to people's crotches! So, I either spend a lot of time nodding and smiling and pretending to be part of the discussion or I have to find the confidence to say, "I'm sorry, I can't actually hear what's going on. Do you mind if we move to the table nearby and you sit and I stand, and we continue the discussion?" Most people are really kind.'

We hold networking events at the AllBright clubs, but we believe in doing them in a different, more intimate way, with spaces to sit, quiet corners to chat, cosy lighting and people from our teams helping to greet people when they arrive and break the ice. It's about making everyone there feel welcome and relaxed.

How to work a network event

- Do your research on who is going to be there and swot up on them
- Have your 30-second elevator pitch ready; end with an ask
- Have your business cards available (sometimes hard if you're wearing a dress with no pockets!)

Online

We spend the equivalent of an entire day online every week, according to research by Ofcom, and with a billion people on Facebook and half a billion on LinkedIn, there's no doubt that online networking is important; in fact, it's often a very useful first step to getting a foot in the door.

Podcast host and author Emma Gannon is an absolute master at building online networks of women. A former social media editor for UK *Glamour* magazine, she now hosts a podcast that has had more than one million downloads, has authored two books, has a weekly newsletter for her fans which has built into a community, as well as active social media accounts. 'Female networks are so important to me,' she says. 'I use private Facebook groups to ask personal questions, for example, and WhatsApp groups with fellow self-employed women where we discuss rates, fees and how to deal with tricky clients or challenging situations. I find that a lot of exciting opportunities and connections come from my newsletter community. It is a smaller network of mainly women (compared to my public Instagram for example) where it feels more intimate, and we can email and share information in a way that feels more personal.'

One-to-one meet-ups

Emma also makes time to transform a handful of those connections into real-world meet-ups, something she says is crucial. We think so too. You might have thousands of Instagram or Twitter followers, but studies show that the maximum number of people you can have a meaningful connection with is 150 (the theory is called the Dunbar Number), so, it's absolutely key that you transform clicks into real-world meets.

Julia Hobsbawm agrees: 'While I am not against the time-saving and scale opportunities of mass personal communications, they are not the norm and we shouldn't forget it. Trust is at its highest in face-to-face settings because we use our senses to really "read" another person. This is why I teach my consulting clients about a "hierarchy of communication". Basically, posting a story on Instagram is not as intimate as suggesting a coffee catch-up with someone you normally "reply all" to on email: try and make some small changes and see a big difference.'

Although our AllBright Academy is a free online educational platform with lots of digital interaction going on between participants during the courses, a lot of the ongoing benefit comes from the Academy Alumni programme, where people meet in the real world to workshop the topics in person. We find that during these in-person meet-ups the conversation naturally flows as there is already a shared connection and experience and the ice has been broken online first.

Maintaining your networks

Meeting people is one thing, but maintaining the sisterhood definitely takes some work. It is hard to keep up with a large and growing network of contacts. Often, in fact, it's impossible. You have to be OK about losing contact with people along the way. This is actually where social media really comes into its own, as it is an easy way of maintaining many relationships even if only sporadically. I use LinkedIn and other social media whenever possible to connect with people I've just met and to see what people who I'm already connected to are doing, and to like or comment when they post something significant. People notice that you've done this and it keeps you in their mind. I know people who are much more active in keeping their network alive and who use their diaries to remind them to drop a quick email or call at certain times in the year. This can be hugely effective if you are in a role or industry where it pays to keep yourself in people's minds. You just have to be organised about it.

Connecting other people who you know, but who don't know each other is a good way of paying forward the networking karma. I usually email one connection to explain why I think they would benefit from meeting the other person, give a bit of background on them and then ask if I can connect them. When I do make the introduction, I give background on each person and context as to why I'm introducing them.

Appoint a board of directors – for you

Once you've built up an extensive network, it's time to narrow that down to your most trusted advisors who can help you steer your career to success. Just as a company would have one, you should appoint a board of directors for your career. This group of people should have diverse opinions and be ready to challenge you – you don't need yes-men or -women.

You can use your business offering to help attract your board. Liv Little, whose network has exploded since she launched the publishing platform gal-dem, to the point where she was invited to run a pop-up shop to support Michelle

Obama's book launch in the UK, has a board of advisors made up of a seriously impressive bunch. It includes the CEO of M&C Saatchi and the partnerships and strategies director at the publishing company Dazed Media. 'It has been so incredibly useful having people to challenge me and develop my ideas. Most things aren't created in isolation, so the team you put in place around you is the most important thing to your success.'

While Liv is at the start of her career, it's something those at the top of their games do, too. 'I absolutely accept that no one is perfect and a great leader surrounds him/herself with people who have complementary skills,' Pam Kaufman says. 'I lean on this group as a team of advisors. I reach out to them for guidance on hiring people, how to handle business meetings and when negotiating any deal.'

The best way to seek someone in your network to ask for advice is to focus on the specific challenge you are facing. Are you about to negotiate a pay rise, are you going for an interview for a new role, are you dealing with a difficult boss or colleague? Then think about who in your network (or your extended network) you know has dealt with this issue. It doesn't have to be in the same industry or even exactly the same challenge. For example, if you're thinking about how to talk to a difficult boss or colleague, it might be a teacher who is the best person to talk to, or a lawyer or someone in the police. These roles involve having to deal with difficult people every day and at the same time being diplomatic and tactful. They may have useful tips and approaches that you can transfer to your own situation.

However, as you start to anticipate their answers, you need to question if you're still learning from your advisors.

'You shouldn't be afraid to bring new people into your sphere of influence,' Facebook's Nicola Mendelsohn advises. And for that, you might need to start networking again.

Sisterhood works

The reason we've put so much effort into our own sisterhoods, and why we want you to do the same, is simple. Men have been networking for centuries, and they've proved that it works. If we want to tap into the top levels of any career, we need to do the same and play the networking game, but on our terms. That's why we truly and passionately believe in the work sisterhood, a group of women (and enlightened men) that can provide counsel, help and support. We know it works because we've seen and done it ourselves.

There's space for so many more women at the top levels of society, government and business – we just have to help each other get up there. We got to the top of our fields with some help from some very supportive women and men, but it's not enough: we want to change the landscape for the next generation of women. This book, along with the thousands of women completing the online AllBright Academy, is our way of doing that and we hope we can inspire you on your journey.

But inspiration isn't enough; it's about taking on board the practical steps that we've detailed in these pages and practising every day. We might make it look effortless from the outside, but we hope that by sharing with you some of the failures and challenges we've both had along the way you can see that it's not. It's still hard, every single day. But the way we get through it, enjoy the work and thrive on the challenges is to constantly lean on each other and our network for support, and more importantly for empowerment and improvement.

We keep working to build the latest version of ourselves as we strive to be better than the day before. The journey is never ending. As soon as you've taken on board the advice in these pages and completed the worksheets, it's time to start again and develop version 2.0 of yourself. Success requires constant work. Lean on your sisterhood to help you. They are your key to success.

Believe, build and then become. We're cheering you on from the sidelines.

WORKSHEET: SISTERHOOD WORKS

The concept of your work sisterhood is vital to every step of your career development, as we hope you've seen throughout the book. Take this moment now to think about your personal board of directors – a very important set of appointments you need to make. Think of five key people in your work sisterhood (and we include enlightened men in this rarefied gathering), write down their names and the topics they can best advise you on or the support they can offer. Make sure you take them out for a drink to tell them of their fortuitous appointment, and what you can offer in return. Remember: networks are circular things and we owe it to each other to help one another out.

1. Who:

_____

_____

_____

What they can offer:

_____

_____

_____

What can you offer in return:

_____

_____

_____

Who can you introduce them to:

_____

_____

_____

2. Who:

_____

_____

_____

What they can offer:

_____

_____

_____

What can you offer in return:

_____

_____

_____

Who can you introduce them to:

_____

_____

_____

3. Who:

_____

_____

_____

What they can offer:

_____

_____

_____

What can you offer in return:

_____

_____

_____

Who can you introduce them to:

_____

_____

_____

4. Who:

_____

_____

_____

What they can offer:

_____

_____

_____

What can you offer in return:

_____

_____

_____

Who can you introduce them to:

_____

_____

_____

5. Who:

_____

_____

_____

What they can offer:

_____

_____

_____

What can you offer in return:

_____

_____

_____

Who can you introduce them to:

_____

_____

_____

Acknowledgements

There are so many people to thank, who have helped, supported and cheered us on over the last few years and during the writing of *Build, Believe, Become*.

First, to our hard-working, inspiring and patient AllBright team, in the UK and the US. Without this group of incredible people we would not have built a business at warp speed over the last few years. Thanks to you all. We hope you're proud of what we're all building and that we don't drive you too mad.

And to our AllBright community. The members of our clubs who have supported us. The women investing in themselves through the AllBright Academy. Our alumni around the world. You have all been part of getting us started and you keep us motivated every day.

Jessica Salter – thank you for your hard work, flexibility and commitment to the cause. Lucy Oates – thank you for working with us and trusting in our vision for a guide to help women supercharge their careers.

To our sisterhoods – for having our backs. To our actual sisters – for showing us the power of women from an early age. To our mothers and to our grandmothers – for being role models and entrepreneurs and for showing us that anything is possible if you believe. And to our sisterhoods who are on tap for us, as we are for them. To Joanna Sellick, Susannah Price, Nicola Shaw QC, Roz Cochrane-Gough, Rashmi Sinha, Tory Frame and Harriet Came. To Nik

Govier, Nicola Blee and Olivia Ross-Wilson (aka 'the cult'), Alexandra Saltissi, Beth Greenacre, Abi Hopkins, Harriet Holgate, Sally Britton and Chania Carr.

To the fantastic women who have shared their stories with us – more than 60 of them. We are extremely grateful to them for their time and their candour. As well as our friends named above who have helped pass on their advice for this book, we add thanks to Naomie Harris, Anastasia Soare, Sinéad Burke, Sahar Hashemi, Antonia Romeo, Kelly Hoppen, Melanie Whelan, Whitney Wolfe Herd, Sue Williams, Georgia Louise, Karen Blackett, Nicola Mendelsohn, Tracy De Groose, Elizabeth Uviebinené, Emma Gannon, Olivia Wollenberg, Dalia Nightingale, Julia Hobsbawm, Cassandra Stavrou, Nicola Elliott, Clare Johnston, Zena Everett, Amisha Ghadiali, Lynda Gratton, Melissa Hemsley, Kathleen Saxton, Lizzie Cho, Isabel Collins, Laurie Nouchka, Liv Little, Cath Kidston, Catherine Baker, Crista Cullen, Michelle Kennedy, Trinny Woodall, Thomasina Miers, Helen Hatton, Nicola Porter, Abi Eniola, Maryam Pasha, Melanie Eusebe, Joanna Coles, Sandy Nunez, Paula Kaplan, Lisa Licht, Katy Koob, Amanda Staveley, Beatriz Acevedo, Nancy Josephson, Pam Kaufman, Marisa Thalberg, Michelle Jubelirer.

To the enlightened men who have supported us. To Warren Johnson for introducing us in the first place. Jonathan Goldstein for his wise counsel and belief in us. Todd Boehly for helping us to crack America. Allan Leighton for his unflappable temperament and perspective. Ben Wosskow – as both brother and business partner. David Kelly as chairman and friend. Kevin Hand for his career sponsorship. To Arnaud de Puyfontaine for his championship and to Michael Rowley for all the support. And to both of our feminist fathers, for helping us to be confident and resilient from an early age. Little did they know.

Debbie's thank-yous

To the start-up sisterhood who were there during the Love Home Swap years, who helped me to go from idea to exit in five years and who were around to workshop, to share and to listen. To Alex Depledge, Kathryn Parsons, Sarah Wood, Caroline Plumb, Karen McCormick and Tamara Lohan.

Anna's thank-yous

To my work sisterhood at Hachette and Hearst, who showed me that a lot of the tips and techniques that feature in this book actually work: Ella Dolphin, Farrah Storr, Eve Burton, Rebecca Miskin, Lara Wilkins, Claire Blunt, Lorraine Candy, Lisa Quinn, Surinder Simmons, Justine Picardie, Sarah Bailey, Jude Secombe. To my EA, Rikki Embley, for her support every day and for trusting me enough to make the leap from that corner office.

And finally, to our families. To Richard and to Marcus. To our children Noah, Gracie, Izzy and Alex. For their love, patience and humour and for keeping it real. They inspire us every day.

References

Introduction

page 1. 'The statistics make for depressing reading ...' Statistics from Jamie Johnson, '"Shocking lack of female entrepreneurs" as it emerges just a fifth of British businesses are run by a woman', *Telegraph*, 21 September 2018

page 2. Data from PitchBook.com, 2017

page 2. Grant Thornton, 'Women in Business: Beyond Policy to Progress', 2018, p6

page 2. https://www.catalyst.org/knowledge/women-workforce-global#footnote32_agfu9zl

page 2. Johnson, '"Shocking lack of female entrepreneurs"'

Chapter One

page 13. 'people who use their strengths every day ...' Peter Flade, Jim Asplund and Gwen Elliot, 'Employees Who Use Their Strengths Outperform Those Who Don't', 8 October 2015 see www.gallup.com/workplace/236561/employees-strengths-outperform-don.aspx

page 19. 'Research by the UK's Corporate Leadership Council ...' quoted in 'Corporate Leadership Council Identifies New Roadmap to Engagement', 11 April 2007 see www.businesswire.com/news/home/20070411005813/en/Corporate-Leadership-Council-Identifies-New-Roadmap-Engagement

page 22. Jack Zenger, 'Developing Strengths or Weaknesses – Overcoming the Lure of the Wrong Choice' see leadership.zengerfolkman.com/acton/attachment/10129/f-0498/1/-/-/-/-/White%20Paper%3A%20Developing%20Strengths%20or%20Weaknesses.pdf

Chapter Two

page 29. 'those who set goals were 33 per cent more successful . . .' 'Study Focuses on Strategies for Achieving Goals, Resolutions' see www.dominican.edu/dominicannews/study-highlights-strategies-for-achieving-goals

page 31. 'Making money and doing good in the world . . .'Arianna Huffington, *Thrive: The Third Metric to Redefining Success and Creating a Happier Life* (WH Allen, 2014) p37

page 34. 'I've never subscribed to the idea . . .' quoted in Emily Cronin, 'Thanks, Mrs Spanx! Meet billionaire underwear guru Sara Blakely', *Telegraph,* 24 July 2016

page 35. 'Emma Stone decided that she desperately wanted to be an actress . . .' from Benjamin Svetkey, 'Emma Stone's Battle with Shyness, Panic Attacks and Phobias on the Way to the Oscars', *Hollywood Reporter,* 26 January 2017

page 36. Commencement Speech 2012 see www.youtube.com/watch?v=ikAb-NYkseI

Chapter Three

page 47. Katty Kay, '100 Women: Katty Kay on how the "confidence gap" holds women back', BBC News, 2 October 2017, see www.bbc.co.uk/news/world-41444682

page 47. Corinne A. Moss-Racusin et al., 'Science Faculty's Subtle Gender Biases Favor Male Students,' *Proceedings of the National Academy of Sciences of the United States of America,* 109, no. 41 (2012): 16474–79; Rhea E. Steinpreis, Katie A. Anders and Dawn Ritzke, 'The Impact of Gender on the Review of Curricula Vitae of Job Applicants and Tenure Candidates: A National Empirical Study,' *Sex Roles,* 41, nos. 7–8 (1999): 509–28; Madeline E. Heilman and Michelle C. Hayes, 'No Credit Where Credit Is Due: Attributional Rationalization of Women's Success in Male-Female Teams,' *Journal of Applied Psychology,* 90, no. 5 (2005): 905–26; Joan C. Williams and Rachel Dempsey, *What Works for Women at Work: Four Patterns Working Women Need to Know* (New York: NYU Press, 2014).

page 52. 'even Oprah has admitted . . .' from Mike Miller, 'Oprah Winfrey Reveals the Problem That Nearly Derailed Her Famous Golden Globes Speech', *People*, 23 February 2018

page 54. 'Just because I'm the CEO of a company . . .' from Ella Alexander, 'How Whitney Wolfe Herd Transformed the Way You Date and Network' *Harper's Bazaar*, 10 November 2017

page 58. '25 per cent of flexible workers who spend time out of the office . . .' statistics from 'Flexible Working: a Talent Imperative', 19 September 2017, see timewise.co.uk/wp-content/uploads/2017/09/Flexible_working_Talent_-Imperative.pdf

page 59. 'I believe we are the best place . . .' see www.sec.gov/Archives/edgar/data/1018724/000119312516530910/d168744dex991.htm

Chapter Four

page 68. 'More than half of digital businesses globally folded' from Leslie Berlin, 'Lessons of Survival, From the Dot-Com Attic', *New York Times*, 21 November 2008

page 68. 'Nasdaq index of technology shares peaked . . .' statistic from Alex Hudson, 'What ever happened to the dotcom millionaires?', 9 February 2010, news.bbc.co.uk/1/hi/technology/8505260.stm

page 69. 'according to a survey by Accenture . . .', quoted in Brian McKillips, 'Why business must hit fast-forward on scaling innovation to stay relevant', 13 February 2018, www.accenture.com/us-en/blogs/blogs-brian-mckillips-scaling-your-innovation

page 70. 'If we're going to challenge the alarming stat . . .', see Claire Cain Miller, Kevin Quealy and Margot Sanger-Katz, 'The Top Jobs Where Women Are Outnumbered by Men Named John', *New York Times*, 24 April 2018

page 73. 'So many people say "I have a great idea" . . .' from interview with Joy Mangano, *CBS This Morning*, 7 November 2017, see www.youtube.com/watch?v=h3Xn02phGPY

Chapter Five

page 91. 'One study showed it even had an effect on your performance . . .' Matthew Hutson, Tori Rodriguez, 'Dress for Success', *Scientific American Mind*, 1 January 2016

page 93. 'According to a three-year study by organisational psychologist Dr Tasha Eurich . . .' Dr Tasha Eurich, *Insight: The Power of Self Awareness in a Self-Deluded World* (Macmillan, 2017)

page 94. 'The trick for introverts is to honour their styles . . .', Susan Cain, *Quiet* (Penguin, 2013)

page 95. 'I remember being in the running for . . .', from Kate Bassett, 'Dame Helena Morrissey: Why it's a good time to be a girl', 7 February 2018, www.managementtoday.co.uk/dame-helena-morrissey-why-its-good-time-girl/women-in-business/article/1456579

page 104. 'A study found that twice as many women . . .', Allison Upton, 'Could the language women use on their CVs contribute to an unequal gender pay gap?', 3 May 2017, www.campaignlive.co.uk/article/language-women-use-cvs-contribute-unequal-gender-pay-gap/1432337

page 98. 'Arianna Huffington has a similar style . . .', see www.lynda.com/course-tutorials/Compassionate-Directness/728373-2.html

page 99. 'a study by the University of Michigan found . . .', quoted in Maia Szalavitz, 'Shocker: Empathy Dropped 40% in College Students Since 2000', 28 May 2010 www.psychologytoday.com/gb/blog/born-love/201005/shocker-empathy-dropped-40-in-college-students-2000

page 99. 'We don't rush our words', Amy Cuddy, *Presence: Bringing Your Boldest Self to Your Biggest Challenges* (Little, Brown, 2015)

page 100. 'Neuroscience research shows that a strong handshake . . .', Steve McGaughey, 'Science Reveals the Power of a Handshake', 19 October 2012, beckman.illinois.edu/news/2012/10/dolcoshandshake

page 100. 'Equinox CEO Niki Leondakis has a powerful nonverbal trick . . .', see www.cnbc.com/video/2018/06/08/the-trick-equinox-ceo-niki-leondakis-uses-to-get-men-to-pay-attention-to-what-she-has-to-say.html

page 102. 'There are scientific studies to back this up ...' http://psycnet.apa.org/buy/2016–55071-001

page 106. 'Optics governed more or less everything . . .', Michelle Obama, *Becoming* (Viking, 2018)

page 107. 'in fact, it takes as little as a tenth of a second', quoted in Eric Wargo, 'How Many Seconds to a First Impression?', 1 July 2006, www.psychologicalscience.org/observer/how-many-seconds-to-a-first-impression

page 108. 'A paper in *Social Psychological and Personality Science . . .*'

page 108. 'subjects were asked to dress informally or formally', M. W. Kraus and W. B. Mendes, 'Sartorial symbols of social class elicit class-consistent behavioral and physiological responses: A dyadic approach', *Journal of Experimental Psychology: General*, 143(6) (2014): 2330–2340

Chapter Six

page 118. 'The budget is not just a collection of numbers . . .', Jacob J. Lew, 'The Easy Cuts Are Behind Us', *New York Times*, 5 February 2011

page 118. 'NastyGal is an interesting example . . .', Eric Johnson, 'What did NastyGal founder Sophia Amoruso learn from failure?', updated 2 Mar 2018, www.recode.net/2018/3/2/17069550/ sophia-amoruso-girlboss-nasty-gal-entrepreneurship-kara-swisher-lauren-goode-too-embarrassed-podcast

page 119. 'Dame Marjorie Scardino remembers being appointed . . .' Katherine Rushton, 'Marjorie Scardino: the softly-spoken American who rose to the top of Pearson', *Telegraph*, 6 October 2012

page 125. PitchBook 2016

page 126. 'But, frustratingly, female angels are in the minority . . .' statistics quoted in 'Study: Women angel investors more likely to give back to female-led startups', 7 December 2017, www.startlandnews.com/2017/12/women-american-angel-investors

page 126. 'women are a better business bet', Katie Abouzahr 'Why Women-Owned Startups Are a Better Bet', 6 June 2018, www.bcg.com/en-gb/publications/2018/why-women-owned-startups-are-better-bet.aspx

Chapter Seven

page 137. 'up to 80 per cent of all GP consultations are thought to be somehow related to stress . . .', from: *The Stress Solution: 4 steps to a calmer, happier, healthier you*, Dr Rangan Chatterjee

page 146. Erin Callan, 'Is There Life After Work?', *New York Times*, 9 March 2013

page 149. 'adults of working age in England . . .', Sarah Brealey, 'Are you sitting too much?', www.bhf.org.uk/informationsupport/heart-matters-magazine/activity/sitting-down

page 149. 'The amount we sit, and its effects, has led to the *Harvard Business Review* . . .', 'Sitting is the Smoking of our Generation', Nilofer Merchant, *HBR*, January 14 2013, https://hbr.org/2013/01/sitting-is-the-smoking-of-our-generation

page 150. 'recently wrote an open letter . . .', Arianna Huffington, 'An Open Letter to Elon Musk', 17 August 2018, thriveglobal.com/stories/open-letter-elon-musk/

page 151. 'This will never be me . . .', quoted in Natalie Gil, 'The Founder of Bumble on the Future of Dating and Making It In Your 20s', 24 November 2017, www.refinery29.com/en-gb/2017/11/179087/whitney-wolfe-bumble-interview

page 151. 'Dr Michael Freeman, a clinical professor of psychiatry . . .', Michael A. Freeman, 'Are Entrepreneurs "Touched with Fire"?', updated 17 April 2017 (unpublished), www.michaelafreemanmd.com/Research_files/Are%20Entrepreneurs%20Touched%20with%20Fire%20%28pre-pub%20n%29%204-17-15.pdf

page 154. 'Arianna Huffington is now the queen of balance . . .', Arianna Huffington and Reid Hoffman, 'Arianna Huffington on Why No One Should Interview While Tired', 8 October 2018, thriveglobal.com/stories/listen-to-this-episode-now *and* Arianna Huffington, '10 Years Ago I Collapsed from Burnout and Exhaustion, and It's the Best Thing That Could Have Happened to Me', 6 April 2017, medium.com/thrive-global/10-years-ago-i-collapsed-from-burnout-and-exhaustion-and-its-the-best-thing-that-could-have-b1409f16585d

Chapter Eight

page 167. 'Everyone gets knocked down . . .', quoted in 'Hillary Clinton to Yale's Class of 2018: "Be ready to lose some fights"', 20 May 2018, www.cnbc.com/2018/05/20/hillary-clinton-how-america-will-navigate-tumultuous-times.html

page 169. 'NneNne Iwuji-Eme, Britain's first black female diplomat . . .', Fleur Britten, 'What She Said: Britain's First Black Female Diplomat NneNne Iwuji-Eme', *Sunday Times*, 15 April 2018

page 169. 'The top Naval Admiral . . .', Tim Ferriss, '5 Morning Rituals that Help Me Win the Day', fhww.files.wordpress.com/2018/09/tim-ferriss-5-morning-rituals.pdf

page 171. 'Creativity is a real journey', Genevieve Fox, 'Anya Hindmarch: "Trust yourself. Life is short"', *Guardian*, 17 November 2018

page 173. 'Eleanor Roosevelt said …', Quoted in Hillary Clinton's commencement speech https://www.themuse.com/advice/hillary-clinton-demonstrates-being-resilient-career-yale-commencement-speech-2018

Chapter Nine

page 190. '*TIME* First Women Leaders: Madeleine Albright', by the editors of *TIME*, http://time.com/collection/firsts/4883068/madeleine-albright-firsts

page 190. Madeleine K. Albright, https://www.albrightstonebridge.com/team/madeleine-k-albright

page 191. '*TIME* First Women Leaders: Oprah Winfrey', by the editors of *TIME*, http://time.com/collection/firsts/4898535/oprah-winfrey-firsts

page 192. 'Music mogul adds her voice to the chorus for a fairer deal', by Anna Nicolaou, *Financial Times*, September 20 2018, https://www.ft.com/content/1d0d70b6-b0ff-11e8-87e0-d84e0d934341

page 192. 'JODY GERSON: WHY I QUIT SONY/ATV – AND STOPPED BEING THE "LOYAL GOOD GIRL"', *Music Business Worldwide*, November 22 2017, https://www.musicbusinessworldwide.com/jody-gerson-why-i-quit-sonyatv-and-stopped-being-the-loyal-good-girl/

page 193. 'Meet Alexandria Ocasio-Cortez, the millennial, socialist political novice who's now the youngest woman ever elected to Congress', by Alexandra Ma and Eliza Relman, *Business Insider*, January 8 2019, https://www.businessinsider.com/all-about-alexandria-ocasio-cortez-who-beat-crowley-in-ny-dem-primary-2018-6?r=US&IR=T

page 193. 'Alexandria Ocasio-Cortez, the 28-year-old who defeated a powerful House Democrat, has an asteroid named after her — here's why', by Dave Mosher, *Business Insider*, June 28 2018, https://www.businessinsider.com/alexandria-ocasio-cortez-asteroid-2018-6?r=US&IR=T

page 193. '*TIME* First Women Leaders: Stacey Cunningham' by the editors of *TIME*, http://time.com/collection/firsts/5380507/stacey-cunningham-firsts/

page 194. '*TIME* First Women Leaders: Stacey Cunningham' by the editors of *TIME*, http://time.com/collection/firsts/5380507/stacey-cunningham-firsts/

page 194. 'MEET THE UNITED KINGDOM'S FIRST BLACK FEMALE AMBASSADOR', by Omolola Ojo, *Nerve Africa*, March 24 2018, https://thenerveafrica.com/16155/united-kingdoms-first-black-female-ambassador-nnenne-iwuji-eme/

page 194. 'I hope this won't be news in 10 years', by Laura Lea, *BBC*, 24 March 2018, https://www.bbc.co.uk/news/uk-43514695

page 195. 'Inga Beale: 'Let's use the words people are uncomfortable using – lesbian, gay', by Jill Treanor, *Guardian*, 23 January 2016, https://www.theguardian.com/business/2016/jan/23/inga-beale-use-words-people-uncomfortable-with-lesbian-gay-lloyds

page 196. 'Lloyd's of London appoints first female chief executive in 325-year history', by Jill Treanor, *Guardian*, 16 December 2013, https://www.theguardian.com/business/2013/dec/16/lloyds-of-london-female-ceo-inga-beale

page 196. 'People regret far more what they don't do rather than what they do', by Emma Walmsley, https://leanin.org/stories/emma-walmsley

page 196. 'Profile: Emma Walmsley, GSK's new chief executive', by John Murray Brown and Andrew Ward, *Financial Times*, September 20 2016, https://www.ft.com/content/c7167916-7efe-11e6-bc52-0c7211ef3198#

page 197. 'The *Guardian* profile: Lady Brenda Hale', by Clare Dyer, *Guardian*, 9 January 2004, https://www.theguardian.com/uk/2004/jan/09/lords.women

page 197. 'UK's first woman law lord appointed', by Clare Dyer, *Guardian*, 24 October 2003, https://www.theguardian.com/politics/2003/oct/24/lords.gender

page 198. 'Marjorie Scardino: the softly-spoken American who rose to the top of Pearson', by Katherine Rushton, *Telegraph*, 6 October 2012, https://www.telegraph.co.uk/finance/newsbysector/mediatechnologyandtelecoms/media/9591486/Marjorie-Scardino-the-softly-spoken-American-who-rose-to-the-top-of-Pearson.html

page 198. 'Marjorie Scardino's rule: how Pearson boss shaped a company and a culture', by Katherine Rushton, *Telegraph*, 3 October 2012, https://www.telegraph.co.uk/finance/newsbysector/mediatechnologyandtelecoms/9585418/Marjorie-Scardinos-rule-how-Pearson-boss-shaped-a-company-and-a-culture.html

page 198. 'Secrets of my success: Liv Garfield chief executive, Severn Trent', by Liv Garfield, *Evening Standard*, 10 May 2018, https://www.standard.co.uk/business/secrets-of-my-success-liv-garfield-chief-executive-severn-trent-a3835876.html

page 199-200. 'About Hillary', https://www.hillaryclinton.com/about/

page 200. 'Text of Clinton's 2008 concession speech', by Hillary Clinton, *Guardian*, 7 June 2008, https://www.theguardian.com/commentisfree/2008/jun/07/hillaryclinton.uselections20081

page 200. '#60 Kiran Mazumdar-Shaw', https://www.forbes.com/profile/kiran-mazumdar-shaw/#60bf265f59ad

page 201. '$800 million biotech business started in a garage', by Becky Anderson, *CNN*, November 15 2012, https://edition.cnn.com/2012/11/15/business/kiran-mazumdar-shaw/index.html

page 201. 'How Spanx Got Started', by Sara Blakely, https://www.inc.com/sara-blakely/how-sara-blakley-started-spanx.html

page 201. 'GM's new 39-year-old CFO Dhivya Suryadevara is making history', by Lexi Churchill, 15 June 2018, https://www.cnbc.com/2018/06/14/meet-general-motors-new-39-year-old-cfo-dhivya-suryadevara.html

Chapter Ten

page 208. Danny Ross, 'Meet the Highest-Ranking Woman in Music Publishing', 25 July 2018, www.forbes.com/sites/dannyross1/2018/07/25/from-alicia-keys-to-ceo-this-woman-is-bringing-profits-back-to-the-music-industry/#2a4960127d7a

page 208. 'I've even interviewed women . . .', Fleur Britten, 'What She Said: Dame Helena Morrissey on How to Ask for a Pay Rise', *Sunday Times*, 19 August 2018

page 209. 'Men tend to be more aggressive . . .', 'What She Said: Amanda Staveley Answers Your Workplace Dilemma', *Sunday Times*, 27 May 2018

page 212. 'women early in their careers . . .', Stacey Chin, Alexis Krivkovich and Marie-Claude Nadeau, 'Closing the gap: Leadership perspectives on promoting women in financial services',September2018,www.mckinsey.com/industries/financial-services/our-insights/closing-the-gap-leadership-perspectives-on-promoting-women-in-financial-services

page 217. PitchBook data

page 217. 'according to a survey by workplacebullying.org', '2017 WBI U.S. Workplace Bullying Survey', www.workplacebullying. org/wbiresearch/wbi-2017-survey/

page 217. 'He would do things like take the rest of the team out for lunch . . .', Fleur Britten, 'What She Said: Mary Portas on Bullying in the Workplace', *Sunday Times*, 4 November 2018

page 217. '2017 WBI U.S. Workplace Bullying Survey', www. workplacebullying.org/wbiresearch/wbi-2017-survey/

Chapter Eleven

page 228. 'Know that you can shift your skis . . .', From interview with Joy Mangano, *CBS This Morning*, 7 November 2017, see www.youtube.com/watch?v=h3Xn02phGPY

Chapter Twelve

page 245. 'Find people who'll make you better', Michelle Obama, *Becoming* (Viking, 2018)

page 254. 'What I hate most is a cocktail reception . . . ', Fleur Britten, 'What She Said: Baroness Tanni Grey-Thompson, DBE on How to Pivot into a New Career', *Sunday Times*, 23 September 2018

page 257. 'We spend the equivalent of an entire day online . . .', quoted in Charles Hymas, 'A decade of smartphones: We now spend an entire day every week online', *Telegraph*, 2 August 2018

page 252. 'Getting to Gender Equality Starts with Realizing How Far We Have to Go', 10 October 2017, www.prnewswire.com/ news-releases/getting-to-gender-equality-starts-with-realizing-how-far-we-have-to-go-300533550.html

Index